S0-BBY-557

Remagen 1945

Endgame against the Third Reich

CLASSIC BATTLES

OSPREY PUBLISHING

Remagen 1945

Endgame against the Third Reich

Steven J Zaloga • Illustrated by Peter Dennis

First published in Great Britain in 2006 by Osprey Publishing,
Midland House, West Way, Botley, Oxford OX2 0PH, UK
443 Park Avenue South, New York, NY 10016, USA
E-mail: info@ospreypublishing.com

© 2006 Osprey Publishing Ltd.

All rights reserved. Apart from any fair dealing for the purpose of private study,
research, criticism or review, as permitted under the Copyright, Designs and
Patents Act, 1988, no part of this publication may be reproduced, stored in a
retrieval system, or transmitted in any form or by any means, electronic,
electrical, chemical, mechanical, optical, photocopying, recording or otherwise,
without the prior written permission of the copyright owner. Inquiries should be
addressed to the Publishers.

A CIP catalog record for this book is available from the British Library.

ISBN-10: 1 84603 249 0
ISBN-13: 978 1 84603 249 3

Page layout by: The Black Spot
Typeset in Helvetica Neue and ITC New Baskerville
Maps by The Map Studio Ltd
3D bird's-eye views by The Black Spot
Index by Alison Worthington
Originated by United Graphic, Singapore
Printed in China through Worldprint

06 07 08 09 10   10 9 8 7 6 5 4 3 2 1

FOR A CATALOG OF ALL BOOKS PUBLISHED BY OSPREY MILITARY AND
AVIATION PLEASE CONTACT:

NORTH AMERICA
Osprey Direct, c/o Random House Distribution Center, 400 Hahn Road,
Westminster, MD 21157
E-mail: info@ospreydirect.com

ALL OTHER REGIONS
Osprey Direct UK, P.O. Box 140 Wellingborough, Northants, NN8 2FA, UK
E-mail: info@ospreydirect.co.uk

www.ospreypublishing.com

These Classic Battles editions are available exclusively through the Military
Book Club

Author's note

The author would like to thank the staff of the US Army's
Military History Institute (MHI) at the Army War College at
Carlisle Barracks, PA and the staff of the US National
Archive, College Park for their kind assistance in the
preparation of this book.

For brevity, the traditional conventions have been used
when referring to units. In the case of US units, 1/179th
Infantry refers to the 1st Battalion, 179th Infantry Regiment.
In the case of German units, 1./Panzer Regiment 7 refers to
the 1st Battalion, Panzer Regiment 7; GR 725 indicates
Grenadier Regiment 725.

Artist's note

Readers may care to note that the original paintings from
which the color plates in this book were prepared are
available for private sale. All reproduction copyright
whatsoever is retained by the Publishers. All inquiries
should be addressed to:

Peter Dennis, Fieldhead, The Park, Mansfield, NG18 2AT

The Publishers regret that they can enter into no
correspondence upon this matter.

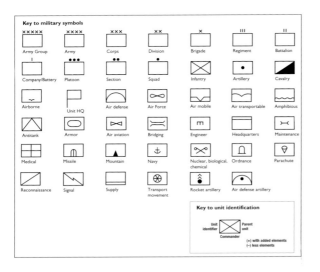

Key to military symbols

CONTENTS

CLOSING ON THE RHINE, 8 FEBRUARY–10 MARCH 1945

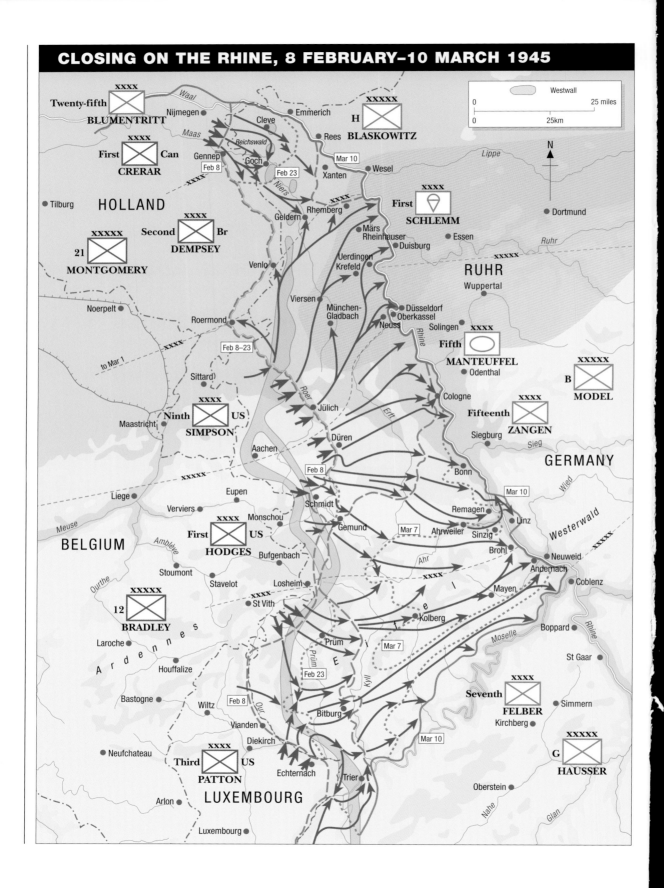

INTRODUCTION

I n March 1945, the Rhine River was the last major geographic barrier to the Allied assault into western Germany. The Wehrmacht, bled white by horrific losses in personnel in the winter of 1944–45, pinned its hopes on the Rhine as the final defense line of the Third Reich. The capture of the Ludendorff railroad bridge at Remagen on March 7, 1945, provided the Allies with their first bridgehead over the Rhine. The capture was a surprise for both sides. The Wehrmacht had been demolishing all the Rhine bridges to prevent their capture and expected that the Ludendorff Bridge at Remagen would be destroyed as had the others in the area. The Allies were already planning major operations to seize a Rhine bridgehead by amphibious assault, but in more favorable terrain north and south of Remagen. The unanticipated windfall at Remagen provided welcome opportunities for the US Army and significantly changed Allied planning for the endgame against the Third Reich. Instead of the deep envelopment of the vital Ruhr industrial region planned since the autumn of 1944, Bradley's 12th Army Group was able to conduct a much more rapid shallow envelopment, trapping Army Group B in the process. Hitler ordered Army Group B to defend the Ruhr instead of retreating to more defensible positions in central Germany, speeding their defeat. The destruction of Army Group B removed the most significant German formation in the west and hastened the end of the war. By early April, Eisenhower shifted the focus of the Allied offensive into Germany with Bradley's 12th Army Group as the vanguard into central Germany rather than Montgomery's 21st Army Group.

THE STRATEGIC SITUATION

The German counteroffensive in the Ardennes in December 1944 had delayed Allied plans to close on the Rhine, but at the same time the costly battles of attrition in January 1945 had decimated the Wehrmacht in the west. The German plight was further amplified by the Soviet winter offensive along the Oder River in January 1945, which forced the Wehrmacht to transfer some of its best forces, such as Sixth Panzer Army, to the east. The Soviet onslaught in Prussia and eastern Germany led Hitler to insist that the primary theater would be the east and that the Wehrmacht in the west would be limited to defensive operations. The defeat of both the Ardennes offensive and the subsequent and smaller Operation *Nordwind* in Alsace had made it clear, even to Hitler, that the Wehrmacht had few prospects for any military miracles in the west. As a result, in February 1945 Hitler committed his last reserves to a hopeless offensive in Hungary. The Hungarian operation was intended to relieve the besieged Budapest garrison and to serve as a

The capture of the Ludendorff railroad bridge over the Rhine at Remagen changed the dynamics of the final battles for western Germany in March and April 1945. This is a view of the bridge on March 15, 1945, from the Erpeler Ley looking westward towards the town of Remagen on the other side of the river. (NARA)

springboard to strike north, trapping the Red Army with a simultaneous strike southward from East Prussia. The offensive was a costly failure and left the Wehrmacht in a perilous state with no substantial reserve of mobile forces to meet forthcoming Allied offensives, east or west.

As Supreme Commander of Allied Expeditionary Forces (SHAEF) in the west, Gen. Dwight Eisenhower had begun to clarify his plans for upcoming operations at the end of January 1945. The Rhine River was the last substantial geographic barrier to Allied entry into Germany's industrial heartland in the Ruhr and the Saar, so planning hinged around this goal. Ever since September 1944, it had been the cornerstone of Allied plans that Montgomery's 21st Army Group would be the vanguard of the Allied push into the Ruhr, first with Operation *Market-Garden* and, after its failure, with a Rhine-crossing operation on the northern side of the Ruhr. This strategic approach had become so widely accepted among Allied strategists that it had become known simply as "The Plan." With the Rhine now within Allied grasp, Eisenhower began to fine-tune the details of how this campaign would be conducted. His intent was to conduct a three-phase operation to breach the German defenses along the Rhine. The first phase of the plan was to close on the Rhine north of Düsseldorf in anticipation of the main Rhine crossing in the sector of Montgomery's 21st Army Group. The second phase was to close on the Rhine from Düsseldorf south, in anticipation of a secondary operation by Devers' 6th Army Group on the lower Rhine. The third phase would be the advance into the plains of northern Germany and into central-southern Germany once the Rhine was breached. Montgomery and the British Chiefs of Staff contested Eisenhower's plans as they favored a single thrust by Montgomery's 21st Army Group, reinforced with US corps. Eisenhower opposed this approach fearing that a single thrust offered the Germans an opportunity to concentrate their reduced resources. A secondary crossing on the lower Rhine forced the Germans to spread out their

The critical first step for the US First Army to reach the Rhine was to first cross the Roer River. Here, GIs of the 84th Division, part of XIII Corps, move up engineer assault boats to cross the Roer on February 23, 1945, during Operation *Grenade*. (NARA)

meager forces and made them more vulnerable to Allied operations. As a concession to British concerns, Eisenhower's formal proposal to the Combined Chiefs of Staff on February 2, 1945, revised the plan so that the main thrust in the north would not be held up by an effort to close on the Rhine in the other US Army sectors. In the event, the US Army was able to close on the Rhine prior to Montgomery's river-crossing operation.

Underlying these arguments were issues of national prestige. By 1945, the British Army was a dwindling force because of manpower shortages, barely able to maintain its current order of battle in Northwest Europe. In contrast, fresh US divisions were arriving every month and by early 1945, the US Army fielded the majority of Allied divisions. Montgomery controlled the equivalent of about 21 divisions including several Canadian and one Polish division. Of the other 94 Allied divisions under Eisenhower's command, 11 were French and 62 were American. On the one hand, Montgomery attempted to guard British interests and prevent the British Army from being pushed off into a secondary mission in the final stage of the war against Germany. On the other hand, Montgomery's lack of fresh British infantry divisions forced him to ask Eisenhower to detach corps and divisions from Bradley's 12th Army Group to make up for shortages to conduct his ambitious operations. In February 1945, Montgomery was still clinging to Simpson's US Ninth Army, which had been detached to his command during the Battle of the Bulge. This transfer of troops from US to British command caused growing resentment in Bradley and other senior US commanders. But at the same time, it reduced Montgomery's bargaining power in dealing with Eisenhower who was growing increasingly weary of Montgomery's insistence on employing the 21st Army Group as the centerpiece of all major Allied offensives. During the debate over the Rhine plans, Eisenhower was taken aside by the US Army Chief of Staff, George C Marshall, and assured that the Combined Chiefs of Staff would accept his plans regardless of the complaints by the British Chief of Staff.

Eisenhower's plan specifically ignored any possibility for a Rhine crossing in the sector of the US First Army east of the Ardennes, the site

of the future Remagen operation. The reason was the terrain and not politics. Moving east out of the Ardennes into Germany, the hilly and forested terrain blended into the rugged and forested Eifel region. Even beyond the Eifel and on to the Cologne plains, the Rhine in this area was unattractive for river-crossing operations as the east bank was edged with high cliffs and backed by more hills and forests. Allied planners remembered the hellish battles in the neighboring Hürtgen Forest the previous autumn and wanted to avoid a recurrence of this bloody nightmare. As a result, Eisenhower's plan anticipated that the US Army would continue its assault on German forces in the Eifel in order to close on the Rhine, but once the river was reached, the focus of operations would be on either side of the US First Army.

The first phase of the Anglo-American offensive began on February 8 with two operations aimed at closing on the Rhine in the northern sector.[1] Operation *Veritable* was Montgomery's effort to push the 21st Army Group through the Reichswald and into position on the west bank of the Rhine for a major river-crossing operation. Operation *Grenade* was a supporting effort by the US Ninth Army to finally clear the Roer River and especially its dams as a prelude to future operations along the Rhine. In late February, Eisenhower approved a First Army plan to assist Operation *Grenade* with a simultaneous crossing of the Roer on February 23 to protect the advance's southern flank.

Operation *Veritable* proved more difficult than anticipated on account of the flooded terrain and stubborn German resistance. With the heaviest concentration of German forces opposing the Canadian and British forces, Operation *Grenade* made far better progress and on March 2, the US Ninth Army reached the Rhine at Neuss. General

A pair of M4 medium tanks from Combat Command B, 2nd Armored Division, cross a treadway bridge over the Roer into the battered town of Julich on February 26 following several days of fighting during Operation *Grenade*. (NARA)

Simpson, the Ninth Army commander, pointed out to Eisenhower that nine of his 12 divisions were free to conduct a surprise crossing of the Rhine. Eisenhower deferred to "The Plan," waiting for a crossing in Montgomery's sector between Rheinberg and Emmerich. The First Canadian Army finally linked up with the US Ninth Army and cleared the area between the Maas and Rhine rivers by early March.

With the first phase of the Allied offensive complete, the US 12th Army Group commander, Gen. Omar Bradley received Eisenhower's permission for the First Army to close on the Rhine. Operation *Lumberjack* began on March 1, 1945, with the aim of clearing the west bank of the Rhine from the Cologne area south, linking up with Patton's Third Army on the Ahr River near Coblenz.

---

1. For more detail, see *Campaign 74: The Rhineland 1945* (Osprey Publishing Ltd: Oxford, 2000) by Ken Ford.

CHRONOLOGY

1945

February 8 Montgomery's 21st Army Group begins Operation *Veritable* to break through the Reichswald to the west bank of the Rhine. The subsidiary Operation *Grenade* by the US Ninth Army is intended to reach the Roer River.

February 23 With the Ninth Army along the Roer River, the First Army is authorized to assist Operation *Grenade* with a simultaneous crossing of the Roer to protect the advance's southern flank.

March 1 With the Ninth Army approaching the Rhine, the First Army is authorized to start Operation *Lumberjack*, aimed at clearing the west bank of the Rhine and meeting Patton's Third Army on the Ahr River to the south.

March 2 The Ninth Army reaches the Rhine near Neuss.

March 4 The 9th Armored Division in conjunction with the 78th Division from the south capture Euskirchen, opening up the Rheinbach Valley.

March 6 Model orders Fifteenth Army to stage a counterattack across the Rheinbach valley to cut off II Corps' advance.
Afternoon Combat Command B, 9th Armored Division, reaches Meckenheim about 15km from Remagen.

March 7
0100hrs Control of Remagen is shifted to 67 Corps even though the headquarters is more than 35km to the west.
0230hrs Major Scheller leaves 67 Corps HQ at Falkenberg for Remagen to take command of the bridge.
1000hrs TF Engemann from CCB, 9th Armored Division, exits Meckenheim for Remagen.
1030hrs Artillery observation aircraft from CCB, 9th Armored Division, sees that Ludendorff Bridge is still intact. Hoge and Leonard decide to seize the bridge if possible.
1100hrs Maj. Scheller arrives in Remagen, minus his radio truck, and takes command of Remagen Bridge.
1320hrs An infantry platoon from the 27th Armored Infantry Battalion supported by a platoon of T26E3 tanks of the 14th Tank Battalion move into Remagen with instructions to capture the bridge.
1430hrs Scheller orders the detonation of the explosives under the western ramp approach of the bridge to delay the US advance.

1520hrs Scheller orders the bridge destroyed. Ignition circuit fails, so a secondary circuit is ignited but only a small portion of the charge detonates. The bridge remains intact.
1600hrs An infantry platoon under Lt. Karl Timmermann reaches the east side of the Ludendorff Bridge and by 1700hrs captures the Remagen garrison in the tunnel.

March 8 Hitler dismisses von Rundstedt and Kesselring takes over as Wehrmacht commander in the west. German attacks against the Ludendorff Bridge begin.

March 11 First two tactical bridges are erected over the Rhine on either side of the Ludendorff Bridge.

March 13 Patton's Third Army launches offensive into the Saar-Palatinate to support Operation *Undertone*; the Rhine "Rat Race" ensues with the collapse of German forces beyond the Moselle.

March 19 The success of Operation *Undertone* prompts Eisenhower to change plans and he gives the green light to Bradley's Operation *Voyage*.

Night of March 22–23 Patton's Third Army makes Rhine crossing near Oppenheim.

March 24 Montgomery's Operation *Plunder* begins crossing of Rhine near Wesel including US Ninth Army's Operation *Flashpoint* and followed by the Operation *Varsity* airborne landing.

March 25 First Army begins Operation *Voyage* to break out of the Remagen bridgehead

March 30 The spearhead of First Army, 3rd Armored Division, engages in a ferocious two-day battle for Paderborn, the last major objective before sealing off the Ruhr pocket.

April 1 Elements of the 2nd and 3rd Armored Divisions meet near Lippstadt enclosing the Ruhr pocket.

April 18 Ruhr pocket collapses, about 317,000 German troops surrender, the largest mass surrender of the war.

OPPOSING COMMANDERS

Field Marshal Gerd von Rundstedt was one of the early casualties of the Remagen Bridge capture, sacked by Hitler a day after the Ludendorff Bridge was seized. (NARA)

Field Marshal Model commanded Army Group B during the Rhine fighting. (MHI)

GERMAN COMMANDERS

Generalfeldmarshall Gerd von Rundstedt led the Wehrmacht on the Western Front as the head of the OB-West (*Oberbefehlshaber West*: High Command West). The architect of the Wehrmacht's stunning defeat of France in 1940, von Rundstedt had been brought back to command the Western Front in the summer of 1943 in anticipation of the Allied invasion. Von Rundstedt was a general of the old school, highly regarded throughout the Wehrmacht for his professionalism and integrity. Although respected by Hitler for his competence, he was outside the Führer's inner circle because of his blunt honesty about Hitler's increasingly delusional military schemes. German forces in the west consisted of three army groups. Army Group H was stationed in northern Germany and the Netherlands facing the Anglo-Canadian 21st Army Group. Army Group B was the largest of the three formations and faced the right wing of 21st Army Group and the US 12th Army Group. Army Group G was located in southwestern Germany and faced the US/French 6th Army Group.

The tactical commander along the central Rhine front was **Generalfeldmarshall Walter Model**, commander of Army Group B. Germany's youngest field marshal, Model was Hitler's miracle worker. When all seemed hopeless and defeat inevitable, Hitler called on the energetic and ruthless Model to save the day. Model had been assigned the hopeless task of re-forming Army Group Center after it was shattered by the Red Army's Operation *Bagration* in the summer of 1944 and, after the Wehrmacht was demolished in France in August 1944, Hitler recalled Model from the Eastern Front and assigned him command of Army Group B. He led the German offensive in the Ardennes in December 1944 and, in spite of its ultimate defeat, he still retained Hitler's confidence.

The German formations opposite the US First Army included Fifth Panzer Army and the Fifteenth Army. On March 1, 1945, there was a switch of headquarters with Fifth Panzer Army headquarters taking over the Fifteenth Army sector and vice versa. The Fifth Panzer Army was under the command of **General der Panzertruppe Hasso von Manteuffel**, the most talented of the army commanders involved in the recent Ardennes operation. The Remagen area was in the zone of the Fifteenth Army, commanded by **General der Infanterie Gustav von Zangen**. He had been an infantry regiment commander at the time of the Polish campaign through the Russian invasion, winning the Iron Cross for his leadership in Poland. Zangen attained divisional command at the end of 1941 on the Russian front with the 17th Infantry Division, which spearheaded the attack on Moscow, and he was decorated with

General der Infanterie Gustav von Zangen was commander of the Fifteenth Army, which bore the brunt of the Remagen fighting. (MHI)

Fritz Bayerlein, seen here while Rommel's aide in the Afrika Korps, commanded Fifteenth Army's limited Panzer force under the command of 53 Corps. (MHI)

the Knight's Cross in January 1942 for his actions in the Moscow fighting. Von Zangen commanded 84 Corps in France in the spring and summer of 1943, and subsequently 87 Corps in northern Italy through the summer of 1944. He was assigned command of Fifteenth Army on August 25, 1944, and led the formation through the autumn fighting along the Siegfried Line, being decorated with the Knight's Cross with Oak Leaves in November 1944.

The corps and divisional commanders were also very experienced, but the emaciated state of most of these formations in March 1945 left them little to command. The tactical commander who played the most prominent role in the later Remagen fighting was **Gen. Lt. Fritz Bayerlein**. He was Rommel's aide in North Africa and commanded the Panzer Lehr Division during the Ardennes fighting. After the Ardennes, he was put in charge of the improvised Corps Bayerlein and during the Rhine fighting in March 1945 he took command of 53 Corps. Since he was the most experienced of the Panzer commanders in the central Rhine sector, Model attempted to shift what little tank strength was available to his command. So for example, in mid-March, 53 Corps was in charge of the central sector of Remagen bridgehead, but at the end of the month when Model feared that the US Army would exit the bridgehead to the north, 53 Corps headquarters swapped positions with the neighboring 74 Corps. Bayerlein's relations with Model were at best, tense, and at worst, antagonistic, Model was apt to be contemptuous of officers like Bayerlein who had spent most of the war on the Western Front fighting the British and Americans compared to Eastern Front veterans like himself. Bayerlein became increasingly frustrated by Model's inflexible insistence on following Hitler's orders, especially when they degenerated into nihilistic tantrums that doomed the Wehrmacht.

US COMMANDERS

General Omar Bradley commanded the US 12th Army Group. Although the group nominally controlled the First, Third and Ninth Armies, the Ninth Army had been subordinated to Montgomery's 21st Army Group for the Rhine operation. Bradley had been one of Eisenhower's classmates in the West Point class of 1913, and both commanders were younger than the subordinate army commanders, Patton and Hodges. He was typical of the meritocratic system of US army field commands in World War II, having grown up the son of a poor Missouri sodbuster and having been selected for the US Military Academy by intellectual promise and hard work. Like Eisenhower, Bradley was a quintessential staff officer rather than a field commander, more comfortable studying maps and planning the logistics of an operation than leading men in the field. Eisenhower tended towards accommodation with British demands in operational and strategic planning, and Bradley played an important role behind the scenes in reminding Eisenhower of US interests in these deliberations especially in early 1945.

The First Army commander, **Lt. Gen. Courtney Hodges**, was in Bradley's shadow for most of the war. Bradley had commanded the First Army in 1944 in Normandy with Hodges as his aide, and when he was

The senior US commanders are seen here visiting the Remagen Bridge after its collapse in mid-March. From left to right are Dwight Eisenhower, the SHAEF commander; Omar Bradley, 12th Army Group; and Courtney Hodges, First Army. (NARA)

elevated to the 12th Army Group command in August 1944, Hodges took his place. Bradley continued to have confidence in Hodges even after his poor performance in the early days of the Ardennes offensive, for which Bradley probably would have sacked any other commander. Hodges was neither as flamboyant nor as aggressive as his neighboring army commander, George S. Patton, but one Patton was enough for Bradley. Hodges' lack of aggressive spirit was partly balanced by the presence of some of the US Army's best corps commanders in First Army, the VII Corps commander, **Maj. Gen. Lawton "Lightning Joe" Collins** and the V Corps commander, **Maj. Gen. Leonard Gerow**. Collins' corps had been at the heart of the US Army's most impressive operations in 1944—the capture of the Cotentin Peninsula and Cherbourg in June 1944, Operation *Cobra* and the Normandy breakout in July 1944, and the destruction of the Fifth Panzer Army spearhead beyond Bastogne in late December 1944. Gerow led V Corps at Omaha Beach on D-Day, but for geographic reasons, his corps played a subsidiary role in the Remagen fighting. Hodges' other corps commander was **Maj. Gen. John Milliken**. He commanded the 2nd Cavalry Division early in the war before assuming command of III Corps. Until recently, III Corps had been under Patton's Third Army, and so the staff was not as familiar with Hodges' command style. Milliken's main problem was that Hodges judged his performance against that of the young and dynamic Collins, a comparison that few corps commanders could meet. Hodges was never pleased with Milliken and sacked him after the capture of Remagen because of his handling of the bridgehead build-up, a controversial decision at the time and since. Major General James van Fleet, previously the commander of the 90th Division, replaced him.

Maj. Gen. John Milliken led III Corps at the time of the Remagen Bridge capture. (NARA)

Of the tactical commanders who would stand out in the Remagen operations, there were many noteworthy examples. **Brigadier General William Hoge** led Combat Command B of the 9th Armored Division that seized the bridge. An engineer by training, Hoge had been involved in the construction of the Alaska–Canada roadway before being assigned to lead the engineer special brigades at Omaha Beach on D-Day, who had been given the thankless task of clearing the beach obstructions under fire. He led CCB, 9th Armored Division, during the legendary defense of the St Vith "goose egg" during the early days of the German Ardennes offensive, one of the key battles that stopped the initial Panzer attack. Many senior commanders thought Hoge was far too talented for his position and that he merited divisional command. He was finally given command of Patton's favorite, the 4th Armored Division, in April 1945. The First Army had no shortage of experienced divisions with excellent commanders.

Brigadier General William Hoge led Combat Command B of the 9th Armored Division during the capture of the Ludendorff Bridge and was given command of the 4th Armored Division in April 1945. (NARA)

OPPOSING ARMIES

THE WEHRMACHT

By the late winter of 1944–45, the German Army in the west was in a state of crisis. The Wehrmacht had been bled white by the Ardennes fighting in December 1944–January 1945 and the Soviet January 1945 Oder offensive. December had been a particularly hard month with nearly half a million German troops killed, the worst month of the entire war. The casualties had fallen particularly hard on the infantry and the pool of replacements had dried up. Increasing numbers of young boys and old men were inducted. Although young boys were supposed to be limited to support roles, Allied troops encountered them increasingly in combat roles as well. Young women were also being recruited for support duties, but as the fighting entered Germany, rear-area tasks such as flak helpers suddenly became front-line positions.

Since Romania had switched sides in the summer of 1944, fuel supplies had dwindled to the point where all but the most essential Luftwaffe squadrons were grounded, aircraft and Panzer training had ground to a halt, and the army was forced back to horse traction. Although German industry had continued to churn out weapons at record levels in late 1944, this did not translate into usable combat power. The larger numbers of weapons being completed hid the fact that it was only accomplished by the reduction or elimination of the production of spares. So tanks sat idle at the front with broken components and little hope of repair, while new tanks sat idle in factory yards unable to be shipped to the front because of the chaos on the rail-lines inflicted by Allied air power. For example, of the 309 medium tanks and assault guns with Fifteenth Army on March 15, 1945, about a third were under repair;

Artillery played an unusually important role in the Rhine fighting since the artillery units were in far better condition than the decimated infantry. Some German artillery was motorized such as this 105mm leFH 18/40 light field howitzer being towed by an RSO tracked prime mover. But the dwindling supply of fuel led to the loss of many weapons like this one, captured by the US Army on the west bank of the Rhine on February 28, 1945, during Operation *Lumberjack*. (NARA)

The bridge was defended by two batteries of 20mm anti-aircraft guns and a single battery of 37mm anti-aircraft guns like that seen here, captured near the Edersee by the 7th Armored Division on March 31 during the breakout from the Remagen bridgehead. (NARA)

a comparable figure for US First Army medium tanks at the same time was only seven percent. A shortage of key metal alloys undermined the durability of high-tech weapons. The final drives of the Panther tank transmission were failing after a paltry 150km because of premature metal fatigue and tank armor was becoming increasingly brittle. The situation bordered on the surreal: the advanced jet engines of the futuristic Me 262 jet fighters were constructed with inferior metal alloys that limited the life of their turbine blades to a few hours of operation so they were towed to their take-off positions using horses because of the fuel shortages that had immobilized the usual tractors.

The units of von Zangen's Fifteenth Army had been badly beaten up in the preceding fighting in the Eifel and had received inadequate reinforcements and little new equipment. Most of the replacements came from nearby convalescent and training units and Gen. von Zangen later referred to them as "either poorly trained, or third-class personnel from other units, most of whom were unfit for service." In early March, the Fifteenth Army had three corps: 74 near Euskirchen, 67 opposite Monschau and 66 north of Prüm. While this might seem like a formidable force on paper, in reality the corps were badly weakened by months of continual fighting and only a shadow of their nominal strength. The 3rd Fallschirmjäger Division had suffered heavy losses in the Ardennes but was the only division anywhere near full strength since it could draw troops from Luftwaffe support units whose aircraft were idle. The neighboring 62nd Volksgrenadier Division had been nearly wiped out at Monschau in early February. The 272nd Volksgrenadier Division had fought in the Hürtgen Forest and the Ardennes campaign and was decimated in the January fighting in the Eifel. The 277th Volksgrenadier Division had still not recovered from its losses in the Ardennes, and it was so short of artillery that two of its batteries were converted to infantry; by early March it was down to three infantry battalions, and on March 8 it had a total infantry strength of only 300 troops. By the end of the Ardennes campaign, the 89th Infantry Division had an equivalent strength of one infantry battalion and at the time of the Remagen fighting it had been partially rebuilt to two infantry battalions and one artillery battalion. Kampfgruppe Botsch was made up from the shattered remnants of four divisions, the 18th and 26th Volksgrenadier, 246th Infantry and 5th Fallschirmjäger Divisions. In reality, each corps barely contained a division's worth of infantry. The situation was so bad along the Westwall defensive line that commanders complained that they had more concrete bunkers than infantry to man them. In view of the badly weakened state of the German infantry, the artillery played an unusually prominent role in the Rhine fighting. The artillery units had not suffered the staggering losses of the infantry, and the morale of the artillery troops was much sounder. Furthermore, the consolidation of several infantry divisions into single battle groups led to a higher concentration of the surviving artillery. The artillery's main weakness was the continuing lack of motorized transport because of fuel shortages, which meant that it took days to re-emplace batteries rather than hours.

The Fifteenth Army assessed its modest Panzer force as having better combat capabilities than the infantry, even though they were badly under strength. By mid-March 1945, 9th Panzer Division was down to 37 tanks and assault guns while 11th Panzer Division had 67 and Panzer Lehr Division had 51. In total, the entire Fifteenth Army had only 309 tanks and assault guns. In spite of the shortage of armored vehicles, the division's Panzergrenadier regiments were one among Fifteenth Army's few reserves of reliable infantry strength and, because of their mobility, the Panzergrenadiers were called upon again and again for local counter-attacks, becoming exhausted and burned out in the process. In total, Fifteenth Army's front-line strength in early March was about 40,000 troops, but von Rundstedt estimated that all of Army Group B possessed only the equivalent of six and a half full-strength divisions.

German Army Order of Battle, Rhine Sector, March 1, 1945

Fifteenth Army	General der Infanterie Gustav von Zangen
74 Infantry Corps	Gen. der Infanterie Karl Püchler
3rd Fallschirmjäger Division	Gen. Maj. Richard Schimpf
272nd Volksgrenadier Division	Gen. Lt. Eugen König
62nd Volksgrenadier Division	Gen.Maj. Friedrich Kittel
67 Infantry Corps	Gen. der Infanterie Otto Hitzfeld
277th Volksgrenadier Division	Gen. Maj. Wilhelm Viebig
89th Infantry Division	Gen. Maj. Richard Bazing
66 Infantry Corps	Gen. der Artillerie Walter Lucht
Kampfgruppe Botsch	Gen. Lt. Walter Botsch
(remnants of four divisions)	

Defense of the Rhine was complicated by the unusual command and control problems that emerged as the German Army retreated further into central Germany. Besides the tactical units of the field army, the German army had a separate Replacement Army (*Ersatzheer*) structure within Germany itself. Germany was divided into 19 military districts (*Wehrkreis*), which were responsible for conscripting and training troops for the field army. However, the military districts also had additional territorial defense responsibilities, commanding local support units such as the engineer units responsible for guarding the Rhine bridges and preparing them for demolition. As will become evident later, the confusion over authority

Severe manpower shortages led the Wehrmacht to induct underage boys and overage men into service in 1945, like these three young prisoners captured by the 4th Armored Division near Berstadt on March 29, 1945. These young boys were often assigned support functions such as flak helpers at the many anti-aircraft gun positions in the German industrial regions. (NARA)

An unusually large amount of heavy armor was employed by the Wehrmacht in the Remagen fighting due to the nearby Kassel plant, which manufactured the Kingtiger. This Kingtiger tank was captured near Mahmecke on April 11 by the 7th Armored Division during the reduction of the Ruhr Pocket and belonged to either s.Pz.Abt. 506 of Panzer Group Hudel or s.Pz.Abt. 507, which supported SS-Panzer Brigade Westfalen at Paderborn. (NARA)

between the field army and the territorial command structure was one of the underlying causes of the problems at the Remagen Bridge.

Remagen was part of Wehrkreis XII headquartered in Wiesbaden, and conduct of defense operations of the Remagen area was the responsibility of Gen. Lt. Kurt von Berg of the Wehrkries XII Nord area headquarters in Coblenz. The district had its own engineer regiment, Landes Pioneer Regiment 12, and the Remagen area was the responsibility of its third battalion commanded by Maj. August Kraft headquartered at Bendorf-Sayn. This unit was made up of older soldiers not fit for regular combat units, often World War I veterans. The engineers were responsible for preparing the Rhine bridges for demolition and were also heavily involved in the operation of ferries to help evacuate troops from the west bank of the Rhine to the east. The Ludendorff Bridge at Remagen was the responsibility of the 12th Company of Ld.Pi.Rgt. 12 commanded by Capt. Carl Friesenhahn, with about 120 men.

The district's two training divisions, the 182nd and 391st, had been committed to the field in 1943–44 because of troop shortages, but there were still other units in the area that were deployed for defense duties in the late winter of 1944–45 such as Grenadier-Ersatz-und-Ausbildungsbatailon 80 (infantry replacement and training battalion). Defense of the Ludendorff Bridge was the responsibility of a convalescent company (Genesendenkompanie 105) from this battalion commanded by Capt. Willi Bratge. This company consisted of convalescent soldiers armed with small arms, nine machine guns and two 50mm infantry mortars and stationed in the town of Remagen, but in March 1945 was badly under strength with only about 35 soldiers.

Since the coup attempt of July 20, 1944, Hitler had grown increasingly suspicious of the regular army (*Heer*), and even his favored Waffen-SS troops had performed poorly in the Ardennes offensive. Hitler was urged by Martin Bormann, the head of the Nazi Party (NSDAP) to put his faith in the enthusiasm and fanaticism of a peoples' army (*Volkssturm*) to master the crisis facing the Third Reich. As a result, in the summer of 1944 the regional Nazi party chiefs, the gauleiters, were given additional responsibilities as Reich Defense Commissars (RVK) entrusted to homeland defense, responsible for raising the local *Volkssturm* militias as well as creating defensive positions in their districts. The RVK were given authority over the "Operational Zone," that is the area 20km behind the front, while the army controlled the "Combat Zone" immediately behind the front. Remagen was part of Gau 18 (Moselland).

The *Volkssturm* was formed under Nazi party control in September 1944, over the objections of the army, which felt that a poorly trained militia would have little combat value. The *Volkssturm* was recruited from any able-bodied men not already conscripted into the military, and so usually consisted of old men and boys. In the case of the Remagen area, a battalion was in the process of formation in March 1945 under the command of Maj. Möllering, a local SA (Sturmabteilung/Brown Shirt) member and Eastern Front veteran. Volkssturm Remagen was armed with 50 French rifles and Panzerfaust anti-tank rockets. As the army feared, it played no role in the March 1945 fighting and simply evaporated. In contrast to its performance on the Eastern Front, the *Volkssturm* played very little role in the fighting along the Rhine. Many of the older reserve officers in command of the young boys were well aware that the war was over and didn't want to waste their lives. For example, in early March a businessman and reserve officer in Bad Kreuznach immediately north of Remagen was ordered to take his company west of the city to delay a US attack. He instead ordered the boys to a bridge over the Nahe River, told them to throw their rifles in the deep part of the river and then ordered them back home.

Although the construction of defensive works behind the front lines was the responsibility of the gauleiters, the layout of the projects was supervised by the army's Eifel High Command (Höhere Kommando Eifel) under Gen. Herbert Lode. In October 1944, local civilians and foreign laborers in the area were conscripted to construct several "blocking positions" with trenches and anti-tank ditches west of the Rhine

To help stiffen the Rhine defenses, armored vehicles' weapons awaiting delivery at local plants were hastily fitted to improvised pedestal mounts to create impromptu anti-tank guns. This is a 50mm KwK 39 gun of the type fitted to the SdKfz 234/2 armored car. (NARA)

including defensive lines near Prüm and along the Kyll, Ahr and Erft rivers. After the late February decision to reinforce the Rhine front, steps began to create a *Pakfront* (anti-tank front) at key points. A number of neighboring ordnance plants had several hundred armored vehicle guns completed but not yet delivered to the main assembly plants, and these were hastily mounted on simple cruciform pedestals to create improvised 50mm, 75mm and 88mm anti-tank guns for static defense.

Since the Rhine area was heavily industrialized and had many rail lines, there were a significant number of Luftwaffe Flak units in the area defending key sites. Remagen was part of Luftgaukommando VI, headquartered in Münster, which controlled an extensive array of flak positions in Düsseldorf, Dortmund, Cologne, Bonn, Essen, and neighboring areas. The heaviest defensive weapons in and around the Ludendorff Bridge were from Luftwaffe flak units. The first two 20mm anti-aircraft guns from 3./I Flak.Abt. 971 were deployed near the bridge in the summer of 1943, gradually increasing to six by the summer of 1944, and located mainly on the east bank around Erpel. A platoon from 5./I Flak.Abt. 715 with 37mm guns was located between Kripp and Remagen on the west bank, though it withdrew to the east bank on March 6, 1945. The 3/900th Flak Training and Test Battalion also defended the Remagen area with a new secret weapon, the Flakwerfer 44 Föhngeräte (storm weapon). This was a mobile launcher firing a salvo of 35 73mm unguided rockets. The most powerful flak unit in the area was 1./s.Eisb.Flak.Abt. 535 equipped with railroad-mounted 105mm flak guns, but this unit was not present at Remagen on the day of the attack. There were a significant number of other flak units in the towns around the bridge as well. These flak units were reinforced by Smoke Chemical Company 160, which was equipped with Fassnebelgeräte 41 smoke generators used to cloak the bridge in the event of air attack.

Young women serving in the Wehrmacht were also captured in increasing numbers as the US Army advanced into Germany, like these captured by Patton's Third Army near Kassel during Operation *Voyage* on April 2, 1945. (NARA)

In theory at least, the field army would take control of all these assorted military formations once the combat zone overlapped the operational zone, but in practice, the changeover often occurred at the least auspicious of times, leading to confusion as would be so evident in the subsequent fighting for Remagen. The field army commanders were very unhappy about the tendency of the military district staffs to interfere even after their areas entered the combat zone. For example, the Wehrkreis XII Nord command was informed on February 26, 1945, that command of the Rhine defense would transfer to the field army command on March 1. Nevertheless Gen. Berg continued to issue orders to local engineer units, contravening orders from the Fifteenth Army staff.

THE US ARMY

In contrast to the deteriorating state of the Wehrmacht, the US Army in early March 1945 was reaching the peak of its combat capabilities. The German Fifteenth Army was facing the US First Army and its three corps, Collins' VII Corps, Milliken's III Corps and Gerow's V Corps. In the ensuing fighting, Collins' VII Corps was mainly involved in the northern sector on the boundary between Fifth Panzer Army and Fifteenth Army, while Gerow's V Corps had only a secondary role in the initial fighting being pinched out along the southern corps border by the southeast orientation of III Corps. As a result, Fifteenth Army's main opponent at Remagen was Milliken's III Corps. On paper, such a contest would seem to pit three German corps against one US corps, but in fact the emaciated Fifteenth Army was significantly weaker than the beefy and heavily reinforced US III Corps. Furthermore, the US Army enjoyed the advantage of continuous air support when weather permitted. The weather in March 1945 was often too poor for close support missions on account of low cloud cover, but III Corps enjoyed the indirect

Among the new weapons first deployed during the Rhine fighting was the M18 recoilless rifle, here seen in action with paratroopers of XVIII Airborne Corps near Münster in late March 1945. Unlike the bazooka anti-tank rocket launcher, the recoilless rifle was designed to fire high-explosive rounds to provide lightweight fire support. (NARA)

advantages of Allied air power in terms of the debilitating effects of air strikes on German rear support areas and transportation links.

The US First Army had fought continuously since the Ardennes campaign, but the mid-February lull permitted units in Milliken's III Corps to regenerate their strength prior to launching Operation *Lumberjack*. The corps contained three of the most experienced infantry divisions in the army, the 1st, 2nd, and 9th, all near full strength. The one new division, the 78th, had entered combat in early December 1944 in the Hürtgen Forest area. It took part in fighting along the Siegfried Line until going over to the offensive following the German attack in the Ardennes. In late January it took part in the attack towards the Roer, capturing the Schwammenauel Dam. As a result, the division was battle hardened by the time of Operation *Lumberjack*. US infantry divisions at this stage of the war had other advantages over their German counterparts in terms of

Much of the fighting in western Germany in March involved close-quarter skirmishes in the numerous towns and villages. Here, armored infantrymen of the 7th Armored Division have dismounted from their half-tracks to conduct a sweep through the village of Memlem on March 30. (NARA)

armored support. Generally, each division had a tank and a tank destroyer battalion attached, usually on a scale of one tank and one tank destroyer company per infantry regiment. Indeed, most US infantry divisions had more armored vehicles than most Panzer divisions at this stage of the war. This enhanced the offensive capability of the divisions. On the other hand, the divisions had been fighting continuously for weeks with little respite, and fatigue was beginning to set in among the front-line infantry.

A single armored division further reinforced III Corps' infantry divisions. The 9th Armored Division had suffered significant losses in the Ardennes fighting around St Vith in December 1944, but by the beginning of February had been brought up to full strength. At the start of Operation *Lumberjack* it had 191 M4 medium tanks (50 x 75mm; 116 x 76mm; 25 x 105mm) and 82 M5A1 light tanks. In addition, it was one of the first recipients of the new T26E3 Pershing heavy tank, a type that would play a prominent role in the capture of Remagen Bridge. Ten of the new tanks were on hand in early March with a platoon in two of its three tank battalions. By this stage of the war, US armored divisions were true combined-arms formations, and not particularly tank centered, as their name would imply. Each division included three battalions each of tanks, armored infantry in half-tracks and self-propelled 105mm howitzers. Unlike the British practice of brigading the division's tanks and infantry together, the US doctrine favored the creation of combined-arms battle groups. Each division operated three combat commands, roughly a brigade in strength, with a mixture of tank, infantry and self-propelled artillery as well as supporting arms such as engineers, reconnaissance and tank destroyers. These combat commands in turn were further divided into task forces, which combined tanks, armored infantry and self-propelled artillery at the company level.

By this stage of the war, most US infantry divisions had attached tank and tank destroyer battalions to provide mobile firepower in the assault. This is a column of M4 medium tanks from the 745th Tank Battalion supporting the 1st Infantry Division on March 5, 1945. (NARA)

Besides the healthy state of its divisions, First Army had an impressive array of firepower support beyond the divisional artillery. In early March 1945, this included four 155mm howitzer battalions, two 155mm gun battalions, a 4.5in. gun battalion and an 8in. howitzer battalion. In addition, the army controlled the 32nd Field Artillery brigade assigned to Collins' VII corps, which included a further two 8in. guns and two 240mm howitzer battalions. All US field artillery was motorized, and it enjoyed the added advantage of sophisticated fire controls netting the batteries and forward observers together by radio through fire-direction centers to concentrate their firepower. An added enhancement was the use of light aircraft, such as the famed L-4 Grasshopper (Piper Cub), for forward artillery observation.

Besides substantial advantages in troop strength and equipment, the weather was beginning to change in favor of offensive operations. Mobile operations in mid-February had been inhibited by melting snow and late winter rain, as well as the consequences of flooding along the Roer River. The weather conditions in March were typical of late winter—light snow mixed with occasional rain, which usually melted and turned the roads to mud. By mid-March, the weather was improving, permitting a freer use of armor.

US Army III Corps, Operation *Lumberjack*, March 1, 1945

III Corps — Maj. Gen. John Milliken
1st Infantry Division — Maj. Gen. Clift Andrus
9th Armored Division — Maj. Gen John Leonard
9th Infantry Division — Maj. Gen. Louis Craig
78th Infantry Division — Maj. Gen. Edwin Parker
2nd Infantry Division — Maj. Gen. Walter Robertson

OPPOSING PLANS

GERMAN PLANS

Operational planning by Gerd von Rundstedt's OB West in the late winter of 1944–45 was largely reactive following the defeat of the Ardennes and Alsace offensives. The drain of the Panzer forces to support operations in the east starting in mid-January 1945 and the massive casualties in December 1944 and January 1945 deprived the OKW of any significant reserves and limited the opportunities for counterattack.

The discussions by the senior commanders of Model's Army Group B favored a timely withdrawal of forces from the west side of the Rhine while fighting a delaying action. The officers saw the Rhine as "a last anchor of salvation." Hitler saw things differently, and pinned his hopes on maintaining a solid defense line along the Westwall. This line consisted of a series of fortified areas created in the late 1930s as counterpart to the French Maginot Line. However, the defenses had been neglected for most of the war, and in some cases their weapons and equipment had been stripped in 1943–44 to reinforce the Atlantic Wall against Allied invasion. Local commanders complained that they had more bunkers than infantrymen to man them, and few held out much hope that the Westwall could withstand concentrated assault.

Model and the senior German commanders expected the Remagen Bridge to be blown up as had all the other major Rhine bridges to that point. This is the Hindenburg Bridge in Cologne, which was demolished during the fighting in the city early in March. (NARA)

Model was distracted from the threat posed to Remagen by the US drive towards Bonn. Here, GIs of the 16th Infantry, 1st Infantry Division, take shelter near a knocked-out Panther tank of Panzer Brigade 106 shortly before German troops demolished one of the last bridges over the Rhine in the city. (NARA)

The First Army exited the fortified Westwall defenses during the February fighting. Here a GI from the 76th Division looks at the damage inflicted on an armored cupola overlooking the Sauer River on February 16, 1945. (NARA)

As a result, German tactics were hamstrung by Hitler's standing orders that no German units were to retreat from the Westwall defense line. Hitler's "concrete tactics" took away most of the Wehrmacht's tactical flexibility and helped ensure a collapse in the defenses on the western side of the Rhine once the Westwall was penetrated as it was repeatedly in late February 1945. Typically, the Allies would focus on a weak section of the Westwall, breach it using a combined infantry-tank force, and then chip away at the shoulders to enlarge the breach. This left German infantry units on either side pinned to the fortifications due to Hitler's inflexible rules. Had they followed this rule, units would have become isolated and eventually surrounded, but in fact many local commanders permitted their troops to withdraw in the event of a serious Allied breakthrough.

To further complicate von Rundstedt's plans, Hitler forbade the army to construct any significant defenses along the Rhine for fear that it would create an excuse for a precipitous retreat behind them. The construction of defenses on the eastern bank of the Rhine was not authorized until February 26, 1945, by which time the Allies had nearly reached the river.

The Fifteenth Army expected that the main threat would be on its right flank with the Americans exploiting the open terrain of the Rheinbach Valley towards the Ahr, which von Zangen described as a natural funnel for military operations. This would inevitably lead the Americans towards the Rhine at Sinzig and Remagen. Model did not agree with Zangen's assessment, and argued that the main focus would be against Bonn. One of the few mobile forces available, the badly understrength Panzer Brigade 106, was moved to Bonn once the US offensive started.

As the Wehrmacht was gradually pushed back to the Rhine, von Rundstedt held out the hope that a defense could be sustained along the river. The river posed a significant natural barrier, but its defense required that the army demolish all the major bridges over the river as they retreated. The destruction of the Rhine bridges developed a peculiar logic in February and March 1945. The Allies made numerous efforts to

As the US Army closed on the Rhine, it became involved in more widespread urban fighting. Here a combined infantry-tank team moves forward in the shadow of the Cologne cathedral on March 6, 1945. The cathedral area was captured that day by elements of the 3rd Armored Division. (NARA)

Operation *Undertone* was aimed at breaking through the German fortified border defenses to close on the lower Rhine. Here, a GI of the 94th Division walks through a gap in a roadblock in Lampaden and past an M4A3 (76mm) of the 778th Tank Battalion that has been knocked out by two gun penetrations through the transmission cover during the fighting for the Saarbrücken bridgehead on March 9, 1945. (NARA)

down many bridges during the winter offensive in hopes of trapping German forces on the western bank of the river. Likewise, German flak units heavily defended the bridges to prevent their premature destruction by the Allies. But as the US Army began to approach the Rhine, air strikes against some bridges were called off in the hopes that a major bridge might be secured. At the same time, the Wehrmacht began to take more deliberate efforts to ensure that no bridges fell into Allied hands. The timing of bridge demolitions by German engineers was absolutely critical in order to permit as many German troops as possible to escape.

German commanders later noted that Hitler's "concrete tactics," the rigid defense of the Westwall, ominously gave way to "court-martial tactics" in early March 1945. In the face of the late February attacks, German tactical commanders began disregarding the orders to stand fast along the Westwall and began withdrawing to the Rhine, sometimes with complicity of the corps headquarters. Model continued to parrot Hitler's orders to hold the Westwall at all costs, and threatened court martial and summary execution of commanders failing to do so. Morale was plummeting not only among the battered and abandoned front-line troops, but among the tactical commanders embittered by the callous orders being received from higher commands.

US PLANS

The Allied late winter offensive was a series of cascading offensives. Following the execution of the Ninth Army's Operation *Grenade* in late February, Bradley activated Hodges' First Army to begin moving forward before the formal start of Operation *Lumberjack* to protect the right flank of the Ninth Army's advance and to secure start points along the Erft River. Bradley's objective for Operation *Lumberjack* was to have the First Army leapfrog from the Erft to the Rhine from the Cologne area south to Coblenz, while at the same time reaching the Ahr River on the army's right flank in order to meet up with Patton's Third Army. The next phase of the operations would be a simultaneous Rhine-crossing operation by Montgomery's 21st Army Group reinforced by the US Ninth Army near Wesel in the north, while Patton's Third Army would make a crossing towards Frankfurt in the south.

The primary instrument of Operation *Lumberjack* was Collins' VII Corps with its three infantry divisions (8th, 99th, 104th) and the 3rd Armored Division, which were facing the Fifth Panzer Army. The focus of the attack was the city of Cologne, with the plan being to seize the city and then turn the corps southward along the Rhine. In the meantime, Milliken's III Corps would advance past Euskirchen to link up with Patton's Third Army along the Ahr River.

The successful conclusion of these operations would leave First Army idle by later in March as there were no plans to conduct river-crossing operations in this sector. Nevertheless, there were a number of bridges still intact in the First Army sector in early March, and some hope that one might be seized. Bradley directed the focus of Operation *Lumberjack* against key Rhine crossing sites. He had little confidence than any intact bridges would be captured, but the bridges were natural congestion points for retreating German units and threats against the crossing sites could either trap larger numbers of German troops or help accelerate their withdrawal by threatening their means of retreat.

THE CAMPAIGN

OPERATION *LUMBERJACK*

The attack across the Erft River by Collins' VII Corps began on March 1, 1945, and proceeded on schedule against ineffective resistance. A cavalry reconnaissance patrol reached the Rhine north of Cologne on March 3 and the main assault into Cologne began on March 5, spearheaded by the tanks of the 3rd Armored Division and followed closely by the infantry of the 104th Division. As was often the case during this stage of the war, some of the stiffest opposition was from heavy flak batteries ringing Germany's industrial cities. In the case of Cologne, 16 88mm guns protecting the airfield fought a violent battle against 3rd Armored Division until being overrun by a tank charge. The 9th Panzer Division, which had been a thorn in the side of the US Army in this sector for months, was finally crushed in the Cologne fighting and its commander killed. By March 6, 1945, the 3rd Armored Division reached the heart of the city near the cathedral and by noon on March 7, the western side of the city had been cleared. All the Rhine bridges in the center of the city had been demolished, leaving Collins' VII Corps parked on the western side of the river for the time being.

For Milliken's III Corps, the attack eastward proved to be a welcome relief from the previous weeks' fighting in the hilly Eifel forests. The gloom and the mud of the forest tracks opened out into the Cologne plains. The fighting on March 1, 1945, centered around Wollersheim where the 3rd Fallschirmjäger Division was entrenched with some

GIs of the 39th Infantry, 9th Infantry Division, mount up on tanks of the 746th Tank Battalion during the advance near Bad Godesburg on March 8, 1945, as part of the effort by the division to clear the Rhine south of the Bonn area. (NARA)

A tank column from the
9th Armored Division passes
through Carsweiler on its way
to the Rhine on March 7, 1945.
The tank in the lead is an M4A3
(76mm). (NARA)

Panzer support. The Wollersheim defenses were overwhelmed by a double envelopment the following day, opening the gate to Euskirchen for the 9th Armored Division. The US advance was further aided by a misconception by Model's Army Group B, which expected that the main objective in this sector would be the city of Bonn. Model attempted to shift the 11th Panzer Division to Bonn to support Panzer Brigade 106 already there. Von Zangen requested permission to withdraw 74 and 67 Corps from the Eifel where they were on the verge of being surrounded. Because of Hitler's standing order to hold the Westwall at all costs, Model refused, but instructed von Zangen that 74 Corps could stage a fighting retreat back towards Bonn once contact was made. In reality, von Zangen's units were in no position to offer any significant resistance, and began to fall back without permission, usually trying to avoid contact with the stronger and more mobile US units. The main road junction at Euskirchen fell to the 9th Armored Division with only light resistance, opening up access to the Rheinbach Valley. On March 5, First Army made some adjustments in assignments, with the 8th Infantry Division moving towards the Rhine south of Cologne. This allowed III Corps to continue its primary mission to link up with Patton's Third Army along the Ahr. On March 6, III Corps attacked down the Rheinbach Valley. In the process, it overran the large ammunition dump at Scheuren that had been supplying most of Fifteenth Army's artillery units, and also captured a significant number of artillery tractors and ammunition supply vehicles, further undermining the German artillery. Late on the evening of March 6, von Zangen gave permission to 74 Corps to begin withdrawing its divisions towards Bonn one at a time

The German Fifteenth Army's position west of the Rhine became untenable. The Westwall defenses had been thoroughly breached and US units were advancing past them towards the Rhine, leaving most

33

A tank column of the 9th Armored Division prepares to move forward from Klembulleshaim on March 6. The weather during early March was rainy and overcast, which limited the amount of close air support available to the US Army. (NARA)

An M18 76mm gun motor carriage of the 656th Tank Destroyer Battalion carries infantry of the 9th Armored Division during the fighting on the approaches to the Rhine on March 7 near Lautershofen. (NARA)

German units isolated behind American lines if they followed Hitler's orders. Instructions from Model's headquarters were increasingly fanciful. The 11th Panzer Division was ordered to sortie out of Bonn and attack the US III Corps on the west side of the Rhine. This proved illusory since by the time the division reached the vicinity, it was out of fuel. Von Zangen ordered Gen. Hitzfeld of 67 Corps to employ the 89th, 272nd and 277th Divisions to strike across the funnel of the Ahr Valley to block Milliken's advance. The attack was doomed from the start. Hitzfeld was actually able to get some of the forces moving by March 6 since they were not in contact with the rapidly advancing US columns. But the country roads were soon clogged with troops, and with little motor transport they were unable to catch up to the more mobile US forces. The units were spared air attack on account of the poor weather and low cloud cover, and the concentration of these forces near the Rhine led to the creation of a pocket of German forces south of Sinzig, trapped up against the river near Andernach.

The Ludendorff Bridge led to a tunnel on the eastern side that passed under Erpeler Ley. Known to the locals as "the dwarf's hole," the tunnel was used as a shelter by local troops and civilians at the time of the US advance over the bridge. (NARA)

This view from the "dwarf's hole" on the Erpel side shows the two eastern stone towers defended by machine-gun positions in the upper stories. (NARA)

Combat Command B of the 9th Armored Division reached Meckenheim by the afternoon of March 6, 1945, and spent the remainder of the afternoon and evening clearing out the town and preparing for the following day's action. Given the lack of strong German resistance in this sector, this placed CCB within a day's march of the Rhine near Remagen and Sinzig. However, the focus remained on moving to the southeast towards the Ahr River. Instructions for March 7 arrived from divisional HQ at 0330hrs and ordered CCB to close on the west bank of the Rhine, capture Remagen and Kripp, secure

A view of the Ludendorff Bridge from the village of Erpel on the eastern bank of the Rhine looking south. (NARA)

bridgeheads over the Ahr River and to be prepared to link up with elements of Patton's Third Army coming up from the south. There was little expectation that the Ludendorff Bridge at Remagen would still be standing, but the daily orders restricted artillery fire against the bridge to time and posit (proximity fuze) rounds to minimize damage to the structure. General Hoge organized his command into two columns with the northern column responsible for Remagen and Kripp, and the southern column for Sinzig.

THE GERMAN DEFENSES AT REMAGEN

German defenses at the Remagen Bridge were fatally flawed because of a confused command structure and a shortage of troops. On March 1, 1945, command of the Remagen sector was transferred from Wehrkreis XII Nord to a new Bonn Sector command under Gen. Maj. Walter Botsch who had been commanding the *Kampfgruppe* of 66 Corps. On visiting Remagen, Botsch was shocked at the poor state of its defenses and requested the reinforcement of the bridge area with at least one regiment, which Model refused since he feared an attack on Bonn, not Remagen, and assumed that the bridge would be demolished before the arrival of US troops. On March 4, von Zangen again pleaded with Model to reinforce Remagen, as it was apparent that the US Army was barreling down the Rheinbach Valley towards Sinzig. Model specifically told von Zangen that none of his troops was to be withdrawn to Remagen and he advised him "not to look to the rear so much."

The Ludendorff railroad bridge had been prepared for demolition in the autumn of 1944 with explosive charges. However, on October 14, 1944, the Cologne–Mühlheim Bridge was totally demolished during an American air attack when a US bomb set off the demolition charges. This led to an order to remove all demolition charges from the Rhine bridges

The detonation under the eastern stone pier damaged one of the steel trusses but the second charge failed to detonate. This view shows how limited the damage was to the bridge. (NARA)

until Allied forces were actually in the vicinity, though the wiring and fixtures remained in place. Botsch ordered that the bridge be charged on March 6, 1945, though it took some time for these instructions to be received and the work did not take place until the following afternoon. The bridge demolitions consisted of several distinct elements. A large charge was placed under the earth approach ramp on the western side of the bridge to prevent access by vehicle once detonated. A series of cutting charges were placed on either side of the main suspension span intended to bring down the main center section of the bridge. In addition, a 200kg charge was placed in an inspection shaft under the main west pier while two 300kg charges were placed at the junction of the east stone pier and bridge structure to undermine both the center span and the easternmost span. There was a separate detonation circuit for the preliminary ramp charge on the western side, and a single detonation circuit for the remaining charges. However, the heavy charges on the east pier had a secondary circuit, part of an effort to create a secondary circuit for the entire demolition sequence that was not completed by the time that US forces arrived.

To further confuse the command situation, on the evening of March 6, Botsch was recalled by Model to take over 53 Corps after its commander had been captured. Botsch was one of the few senior officers to have first-hand knowledge of the confused command structure around the bridge, and responsibility for the bridge was transferred to Gen. Otto Hitzfeld's 67 Corps at 0100hrs on March 7. Unfortunately, Hitzfeld's headquarters was at Falkenberg more than 35km from the bridge, in fact more than double the distance of the lead elements of the US 9th Armored Division which were less than 15km from the bridge. Hitzfeld had been ordered to stage an attack against the 9th Armored Division that day to cut off the assault down the Rheinbach Valley, and when he suggested diverting his meager forces to defend Remagen instead, he was categorically told to stick to the attack. Hitzfeld realized that the attack

GERMAN UNITS
Fifth Panzer Army
58 Panzer Corps
A 12th Volksgrenadier Division
B 353rd Infantry Division

Fifteenth Army
74 Corps
C 3rd Fallschirmjäger Division
D 272nd Volksgrenadier Division
E 62nd Infantry Division

67 Corps
F 277th Volksgrenadier Division
G 89th Infantry Division
H Bonn Command
I Panzer Brigade 106

First HODGES

III MILLIKEN

V GEROW

DUREN

WOLLERSHEIM

▼ EVENTS

1. **3rd Fallschirmjäger Division defends Wollersheim on March 1 against repeated attacks by CCA, 9th Armored Division.**

2. **The 52nd Armored Infantry Battalion, CCA, 9th Armored Division, and a battalion from the 310th Infantry, 78th Division, encircle and take Wollersheim.**

3. **General Püchler tries to stem the American breakthrough with a *Kampfgruppe* from the 62nd Infantry Division, but the attack is so weak that the US forces hardly notice it.**

4. **The 1st Infantry Division advances over the Erft River against little resistance on March 2, but has a tough fight for Erp, which doesn't fall until March 3.**

5. **The CCB, 9th Armored Division, crosses the Erft on March 2 north of Euskirchen.**

6. **Euskirchen is taken on March 4 by a combined attack of CCA, 9th Armored Division, on the northern side and the 78th Division from the south.**

7. **On March 5, the 9th Infantry Division is ordered to seal off Bonn from the south at Bad Godesberg which it reaches on March 7.**

8. **The 1st Infantry Division is directed to take Bonn and reaches the outskirts of the city after dark on March 7.**

9. **Ahrweiler is taken in the early evening of March 7 by the 78th Division, placing the division on the Ahr River.**

10. **The CCB, 9th Armored Division reaches Meckenheim on afternoon of March 6.**

11. **Around midnight on March 6/7, Model orders 67 Corps to defend westward with the 89th Division while staging a counterattack across the Rheinbach Valley towards Gelsdorf using the 272nd and 277th Volksgrenadier Divisions.**

12. **In the early morning hours of March 7, 67 Corps is given responsibility for the Remagen area from Bonn Command; Gen. Hitzfeld sends his aide, Maj. Scheller to take command of the Ludendorff Bridge.**

13. **The CCB, 9th Armored Division, is ordered to close on the Ahr River in the early morning hours of March 7, sending one task force towards Remagen and the other towards Sinzig.**

14. **Task Force Engeman, CCB, 9th Armored Division, reaches the heights over Remagen in the late morning of March 7 and sees that the Ludendorff Bridge is still intact**

OPERATION *LUMBERJACK*, MARCH 1–7, 1945

The III Corps advance on Remagen

Note: Gridlines are shown at intervals of 5km (3.10 miles)

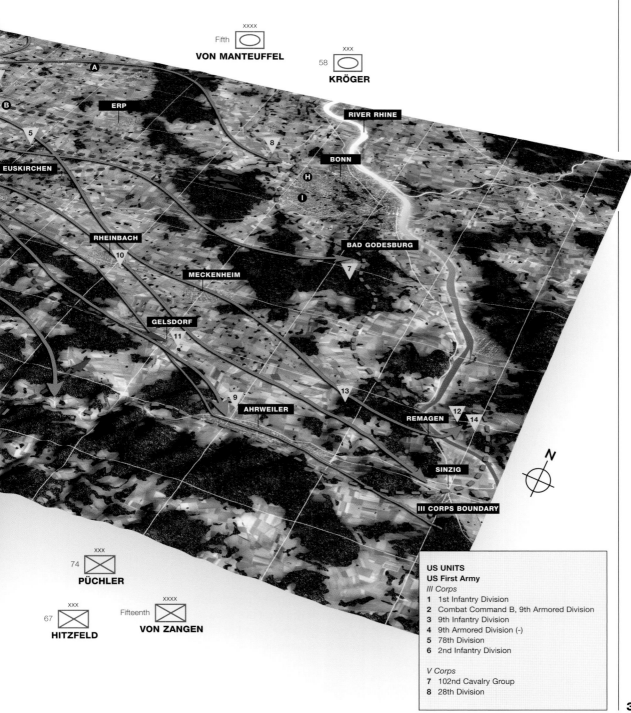

Fifth **VON MANTEUFFEL**

58 **KRÖGER**

A

B

ERP

RIVER RHINE

5

EUSKIRCHEN

8

BONN

H

I

RHEINBACH

10

BAD GODESBURG

MECKENHEIM

7

GELSDORF

11

13

9

AHRWEILER

12

REMAGEN

14

SINZIG

N

III CORPS BOUNDARY

74 **PÜCHLER**

67 **HITZFELD**

Fifteenth **VON ZANGEN**

US UNITS
US First Army

III Corps
1 1st Infantry Division
2 Combat Command B, 9th Armored Division
3 9th Infantry Division
4 9th Armored Division (-)
5 78th Division
6 2nd Infantry Division

V Corps
7 102nd Cavalry Group
8 28th Division

Among the weapons defending the bridge was the secret Flakwerfer 44 Föhngeräte of the 900th Flak Training and Test Battalion stationed on both sides of the river. This example was captured in Erpel and behind it is a US Army M16 anti-aircraft half-track of the 634th AAA Battalion (Automatic Weapon) guarding the bridge area. (NARA)

order was complete fantasy since his units were isolated far behind the American spearhead, and he feared that if Remagen remained exposed, the bridge would be demolished at the first sign of the Americans, leaving his corps trapped on the west bank of the Rhine. At 0130hrs, he instructed his aide-de-camp, Maj. Hans Scheller, to take a vehicle and a communications truck to Remagen, take command of the bridge and establish a defensive perimeter with any troops available. He made it clear to Scheller that under no circumstances was the bridge to fall into American hands, but on the other hand, he also made it clear that the Ludendorff Bridge was the best hope for the retreat of his comrades in 67 Corps. Scheller set off around 0230hrs in a confident mood, remarking to one staff officer that it was a "Knight's Cross mission." Little did he realize the tragedy that awaited.

Since no ground attack had been anticipated against the Ludendorff Bridge, German combat forces around it were minimal. Although there were about 1,000 troops in the vicinity of the bridge, nearly all were support troops. The main units assigned to the bridge were Friesenhahn's 12th Company of Landes Pioneer Regiment 12, numbering about 120 troops, and Bratge's Convalescent Company 105 with 36 men. Captain Willi Bratge had been the Remagen commander since December 1944 and was a thrice-wounded veteran of the Polish and French campaign, invalided out because of wounds suffered in Russia.

There were three flak batteries around the bridge, including 20mm batteries located on Erpel Hill overlooking the bridge from the eastern side, and a 37mm battery that had retreated from the western side under murky circumstances the day before. Besides these units in the Remagen area, there were about 150 Hitler Youth serving mainly as "flak helpers," two companies of untrained *Volkssturm* and a number of railroad and construction troops. There had been a significant number of other units that had congregated in the Remagen area in early March on account of the American advance, but before Bratge could organize them to defend the bridge, on the night of March 5–6 they retreated across the bridge and disappeared without informing him. The situation so alarmed Bratge that on March 7 he telephoned Army Group B headquarters. At the time, Model and his staff were on the road to a new location, and the duty officer reassured Bratge that he had nothing to fear and that American actions were expected to concentrate against Bonn and not his bridge. Neither Army Group B headquarters nor Fifteenth Army knew that Maj. Scheller was on his way to take command of the defenses.

Scheller finally arrived at Remagen at 1100hrs on May 7 though the radio truck had gotten lost on the way. As a result, Remagen was cut off from any higher command authorities since there were no tactical radios at the bridge, and telephone contact was sporadic at best.

THE AMERICAN ADVANCE ON REMAGEN

Lieutenant Colonel Leonard Engeman of the 14th Tank Battalion led Task Force Engeman, the northern column of CCB, 9th Armored Division. This column was assigned the task of clearing Remagen and Kripp while the southern column was aimed at securing river crossings over the Ahr near Sinzig further south. Engeman's column did not manage to set off on its mission on March 7, 1945, until 1000hrs due to all the rubble blocking the roads around Meckenheim from the previous air attacks. The column was organized in the following order:

Task Force Engeman (Northern Column, CCB, 9th Armored Division), March 7, 1945

1st Platoon, Company A, 14th Tank Battalion
Company A, 27th Armored Infantry Battalion
Engineer platoon, Company B, 9th Armored Engineer Battalion
Company C, 27th Armored Infantry Battalion
Assault Gun Platoon, 27th Armored Infantry Battalion
Mortar Platoon, 27th Armored Infantry Battalion
Command Section, 27th Armored Infantry Battalion
Company A, 14th Tank Battalion (-)
Mortar Platoon, 14th Tank Battalion
Company B, 27th Armored Infantry Battalion
Assault Gun Platoon, 14th Tank Battalion
Command Section, 14th Tank Battalion
Company D, 14th Tank Battalion.

Around 1030hrs, a Piper Cub spotting for the divisional artillery flew over the fog-shrouded bridge, and saw it was still standing. When informed of this, Hoge conferred with the divisional commander, Maj. Gen. John Leonard, in Meckenheim to discuss what course of action should be taken if TF Engeman found the bridge still intact when it arrived. The main mission was to close on the Ahr River and there were no instructions from III Corps about any effort to seize a bridgehead. They both decided that the opportunity should be taken if the Germans were foolish enough to leave the bridge intact. For security reasons, Hoge didn't want the new instructions sent by radio, so one of the staff officers, Maj. Ben Cothran, set off in a jeep for Engeman's column with orders to take the bridge if it was still standing.

By the time Cothran reached Engeman's column, the lead elements had already cleared the woods west of Remagen and were sitting on a hilltop clearing overlooking the bridge. Not only was the bridge still standing, but there was also traffic moving across it as well as considerable activity along the rail-line along the eastern bank. Engeman looked over the terrain and decided to send in the infantry of Company A, 27th Armored Infantry Battalion, on foot, followed by Lt. John Grimball's platoon of T26E3 tanks from the 14th Tank Battalion for support. The infantry set off down the hill at 1320hrs followed by the tanks. Neither Bratge's company nor the *Volkssturm* offered any serious resistance and the town of Remagen appeared mostly deserted.

Shortly after Scheller took over the command of the German defenses at Remagen, the first reports began to arrive around 1120hrs that American tanks were moving towards the town. Bratge immediately suggested that the bridge be demolished. With no Americans yet in view,

The attack on the Ludendorff Bridge was supported by a platoon of the new T26E3 Pershing tanks led by Lt. Grimball of the 14th Tank Battalion. This is one of the platoon's tanks seen on March 1 with its turret traversed to the rear in travel mode. (NARA)

A number of these modified PaK 43/3 88mm guns were knocked out by the new Pershing tanks of the 9th Armored Division on the approaches to the Rhine. These weapons were intended for the Jagdpanther tank destroyer, but instead were adapted to a pedestal mount for use as an improvised anti-tank gun for Rhine defense. (NARA)

Scheller urged patience since he did not want to demolish the bridge prematurely and trap his corps on the west bank. Around noon, the bridge commander, Capt. Carl Friesenhahn, also suggested to Scheller that the bridge be destroyed immediately. Scheller instructed the engineers to complete preparations for demolition, but instructed Friesenhahn to await his instructions before actually initiating the demolition sequence. About this time, Lt. Karl Peters, commanding a Luftwaffe flak battery armed with the secret new Flakwerfer 44 rocket weapon, arrived and informed Scheller that their units would soon arrive to cross the bridge. A horse-drawn artillery battalion also appeared so Scheller had the engineers remove landmines emplaced on the bridge to clear a passage.

Around 1300hrs, the German officers on the Erpel side of the bridge heard the first rifle shots from Remagen as the US infantry began to enter the town from the direction of the Apollinaris church on the hill to the north of the town. Friesenhahn again asked permission to detonate the bridge. Through binoculars, Scheller could see no evidence of US troops and again refused. By 1400hrs, Friesenhahn's troops had completed their work preparing the main detonation circuit for the demolition charges, though the secondary circuit was still not complete. With this task accomplished, Scheller and Friesenhahn set off for the western side of the bridge, reaching a neighboring lumberyard around 1430hrs. The German engineer troops tested the firing circuit and found that it was still operating properly.

The lead elements of TF Engeman had passed through Remagen with very little fighting. The tanks and infantry took separate routes along parallel streets, finally meeting near the approach embankment to the railroad bridge. Grimball's tank platoon reached the bridge ramp around the same time as Scheller's party. Engeman radioed Grimball to cover the bridge with fire and to knock out the two locomotives active on the eastern side of the river. Hoge was also watching the progress of the spearhead from an overlying hill and ordered the mortar and assault gun

The infantry advance over the bridge was led by Lt. Karl Timmermann from Company A, 27th Armored Infantry Battalion. (NARA)

A reconnaissance unit of the 9th Armored Division passes through Remagen. The Nazi party stepped up its propaganda efforts in the final months of the war and the slogan on the wall reads "Those listening to enemy radio and rumor-mongers are traitors to the nation and are as good as dead." (NARA)

Infantry of the 78th Division ride on tanks of the 741st Tank Battalion through the streets of Remagen on March 9 during the efforts to reinforce the bridgehead. (NARA)

platoons to cover the bridge with smoke to facilitate an infantry attack over it. As Grimball's tanks cleared the buildings near the bridge, they came under fire from flak guns on the Erpel hill, but with little effect.

Shortly after Scheller and Friesenhahn reached the western side of the Ludendorff Bridge, they heard the sound of whistles and the infantry of Company A, 27th Armored Infantry Battalion, began to race towards the bridge. Friesenhahn ordered the detonation of a preliminary charge under the approach ramp and both officers and the other members of their party scurried back over the bridge. The detonation created a large crater on the bridge ramp that was deep enough to stop vehicles from reaching the bridge, but which would not stop determined infantry.

Once the dust and debris settled down near the approach ramp, it became clear to Grimball that tanks would not be able to make it on to the bridge until the crater was filled. Hoge ordered Major Deevers, the commander of the 27th Armored Infantry Battalion, to send a company of infantry across, and Engeman told Lt. Hugh Mott, leading a platoon from Company B, 9th Armored Engineer Battalion, to follow them on the bridge and deal with any further demolition charges.

During their run back over the bridge, Friesenhahn became separated from Scheller when a projectile landed near him and knocked him momentarily unconscious. By the time that he arrived back on the eastern side of the bridge the instructions to detonate the main charges had still not been given. The area in front of the tunnel was targeted by US fire, and it took a few moments before Friesenhahn and Bratge could find Scheller in the tunnel to obtain permission to blast the bridge. Around 1520hrs, Scheller finally shouted to Friesenhahn to "blow the bridge" and the engineer captain went to the main detonator near the tunnel entrance. To his dismay, the device did not work even after a few attempts. With the main demolition circuit inoperable, Friesenhahn realized that the only way to prevent the American advance over the bridge was to trigger a partial secondary circuit connected to the charges at the eastern stone pier of the bridge. A volunteer, Corporal Anton Faust

Following the bridge capture, the First Army rapidly pushed troops over the bridge to create a viable bridgehead on the eastern bank of the river. Here, a column of M4 medium tanks is seen moving to the eastern bank on March 11. (NARA)

set off from the shelter of the tunnel to the triggering device about 80m away, ignited the primer charge and ran back towards the tunnel.

Lt. Karl Timmermann of Company A led the US infantry advance over the bridge and, before they started across the bridge, the charge under the eastern pier detonated. The US infantry did not know that this was not the full demolition charge and expected the whole bridge to collapse. When the smoke settled, the bridge was still intact. The back-up charge consisted of two charges on either side but only the southern one went off, and the Donarit commercial explosive did not prove potent enough to scuttle the bridge itself. US engineers later discovered that the blasting cap in the second charge had gone off, but it had not been placed deeply enough in the explosives to detonate the main charge.

It took considerable prodding from Timmermann to get his three infantry platoons onto the bridge, as there was the understandable fear that another explosion would soon follow and demolish the remaining structure. The infantry platoons advanced cautiously and slowly over the bridge and began receiving machine-gun fire from Friesenhahn's troops in the two towers on the eastern side of the structure. On reaching the center of the bridge, they also began to receive machine-gun fire from a barge positioned on the river. This barge was hit by tank gunfire from the western bank, ending this source of fire; the tanks also engaged the two towers. The flak batteries on the Erpeler Ley tried to fire against the bridge, but many of the batteries did not have enough depression to fire downward. As the American infantry advanced across the bridge, the US engineers began removing explosive charges under the bridge decking and dropping them into the Rhine below. Casualties were light, with apparently only one wounded.

Sergeant Joseph DeLisio was in the lead of the advancing 3rd Platoon and broke into one of the two eastern towers. He captured the three-

US UNITS

1. 3rd Platoon, Company C, 27th Armored Infantry, 9th Armored Division
2. Heavy Tank Platoon, Co. A, 14th Tank Battalion, 9th Armored Division
3. Company A, 27th Armored Infantry, 9th Armored Division
4. Company B, 27th Armored Infantry, 9th Armored Division
5. Company C, 27th Armored Infantry, 9th Armored Division
6. 310th Infantry, 78th Division

9 **CRAIG**

REMAGEN

ERPEL

LUDENDORFF BRIDGE

▼ EVENTS

1. **Lieutenant Karl Timmermann's 3rd Platoon, Company C, 27th Armored Infantry, approaches the bridge around 1415hrs.**

2. **Lieutenant John Grimball's T26E3 Pershing tanks from the 14th Tank Battalion meet the infantry and proceed to the bridge.**

3. **Major Scheller's party reaches lumber yard on western side of the river around 1430hrs.**

4. **On hearing US infantry approaching, Scheller's party races back over the bridge and detonates the preliminary charge under the western bridge approach at around 1440hrs.**

5. **A US tank-infantry team reaches the bridge around 1500hrs, and is temporarily halted by blown approach ramp.**

6. **Scheller, back in the "Dwarf's Hole" tunnel, orders the demolition of the bridge at 1520hrs.**

7. **The detonation circuit fails, Cpl. Anton Faust volunteers to leave the tunnel and set off the secondary circuit.**

8. **The secondary circuit detonates the charge under the southeast pier, but the bridge remains intact.**

9. **Timmermann's platoon begins a cautious advance over the bridge.**

10. **Flak positions on Erpeler Ley bring US troops under fire.**

11. **Machine-gun positions on the eastern towers fire on the approaching US troops; they are quickly captured.**

12. **Timmerman's platoon is over the river by 1600hrs.**

13. **Company B and parts of Company A, 27th Armored Engineers, climb Erpeler Ley and capture the flak positions.**

14. **Company C takes up defensive positions in Erpel.**

15. **Timmermann and troops from Company A reach the eastern side of the "Dwarf's Hole" around 1700hrs where bridge garrison surrenders.**

16. **Major Strobel despatches about 100 engineers and flak crew to retake the bridge or destroy it.**

17. **In the pre-dawn hours, the German counterattack is stopped by the newly arrived 310th Infantry, 78th Division, and other US troops who have moved over the bridge that evening.**

REMAGEN, MARCH 7/8, 1945

The capture of the Ludendorff Bridge

Note: Gridlines are shown at intervals of 250m (273.4 yds)

xxx
67 HITZFELD

15

4

ERPELER LEY 10 13
D

6

12

6

17

16

RIVER RHINE

N

GERMAN UNITS
A Volkssturm Remagen-Kripp
B Convalescent Company 105
C Company 12, Landes Pioneer Regiment 12
D 20mm Flak battery 3./l.Flak.Abt. 971
E 37mm Flak battery 5./l.Flak.Abt. 715

man machine-gun squad and an observation team, and escorted them out of the tower. His platoon cleared the other tower and continued to advance towards the eastern side of the bridge. The first soldier across was Sgt. Alex Drabik, followed shortly after by the rest of the company and Lt. Timmermann. There was little resistance from German troops other than those in the towers, and most had fled into the tunnel. Friesenhahn and Bratge tried to rally the assorted troops cowering inside but could not make them budge. In the confusion, Maj. Scheller took a bicycle and escaped out of the eastern side of the tunnel to report the loss of the bridge to higher headquarters since they had no contact by either telephone or radio. Timmermann, DeLisio, Mott and Drabik were among the several 9th Armored Division troops awarded the Distinguished Service Cross for their actions at Remagen.

Timmermann realized that the high ground over the tunnel had to be secured to ensure the security of the bridgehead and directed his company to begin the climb while a small number of troops guarded the tunnel entrance. The fight for the Erpeler Ley, known to the Americans as "Flak Hill," was far more costly than the advance over the bridge. The hill was steep and covered at parts with loose stone. A number of US infantrymen were critically injured when they slipped on the stone and fell. As they reached the peak, they became exposed to the 20mm flak guns positioned on the hill. With the help of supporting tank gunfire, the hill was cleared and Timmermann and a small number of infantrymen made their way to the eastern exit of the tunnel around 1700hrs.

Inside the tunnel, Friesenhahn asked for a volunteer to escape and inform higher headquarters of the loss of the bridge. With no radio or telephones available, he assigned the soldier a motorcycle. As the motorcyclist sped out of the main tunnel entrance near the bridge, he was brought under a hail of gunfire from US infantry and finally felled by a burst of machine-gun fire. With Scheller missing, Bratge took command and attempted to rally the troops around the eastern tunnel exit. He

A pair of M16 multiple-gun motor carriages guard the western side of the Ludendorff Bridge against Luftwaffe air attack. Reinforcing the anti-aircraft defenses of the bridge was one of the US Army's primary efforts immediately after the bridge's capture. (NARA)

The rapid reinforcement of the bridgehead stymied early German counterattacks. The early arrival of a battalion from the 78th Division halted the attack by a German engineer battlegroup in the pre-dawn hours of March 8. Here, a fire team from the division prepares to go on patrol near the bridge. (NARA)

Engineer units were hastily dispatched to Remagen to help construct additional tactical bridges. This is a column from the 552nd Engineer Heavy Pontoon Battalion on the road into Remagen on March 10 bringing in pontoons that were used to create the first tactical bridges there. (NARA)

had no idea that Timmermann and his men had already reached the exit. The troops were intermingled with terrified civilians, and some began to wander out the tunnel entrance waving white flags. Assuming that the troops in the tunnel were surrendering, US infantry began to enter, shouting at the Germans. Bratge realized that the situation was hopeless and instructed the officers around him to lay down their arms. The Ludendorff Bridge and its garrison were now in American hands.

One of the lingering mysteries of the capture of the Ludendorff Bridge is why the explosive charges failed to detonate. Counterintelligence officers of the 9th Armored Division later interrogated some of the German officers, civilians and foreign laborers captured in the tunnel. Friesenhahn said that he thought the main cable had been hit by tank fire; an unlikely event but certainly not impossible. One of the Polish forced

US Army engineers attempt to repair the damage caused to the bridge by the detonation of one of the charges under the eastern pier. This area was further damaged on the night of March 7–8 when a US tank destroyer slipped into the gap while crossing the bridge. (NARA)

laborers and at least two disgruntled German soldiers claimed they had sabotaged the circuit, but the circuit had been last tested that afternoon and had worked. So it is possible that the charge was rendered ineffective by sabotage at the last moment, by inexperienced engineers setting the charges improperly, by tank fire against the bridge, or a combination of factors. There was no positive way to determine the cause as US engineers had ripped up much of the detonation circuit during the capture of the structure.

REACTION TO THE BRIDGE CAPTURE

The Wehrmacht reacted to the bridge capture much more slowly and haphazardly than the US Army. The German command network was chaotic as many officers were in transit to new headquarters and did not learn of the capture for many hours after the bridge was seized. In contrast, the 9th Armored Division passed word along the chain of command from Gen. Hodges to Gen. Bradley almost immediately. As a result, the US Army began reinforcing the bridgehead that evening while German actions were mainly confined to local initiatives.

Bradley contacted Eisenhower and he quickly agreed that the bridgehead had to be reinforced as rapidly as possible. The mission to link up First and Third Armies remained, but the immediate priority became the transfer of units to defend the bridge. CCB, 9th Armored Division, was relieved of its mission towards the Ahr River and ordered to move as many troops as possible over the river. At the same time neighboring units were scoured for troops to rush to the bridge, including two infantry regiments from the 78th Division and a battalion from the 9th Infantry Division. The 14th Tank Battalion began sending tanks over after nightfall, as soon as the engineers deemed the bridge safe. In the early hours of March 8, a tank destroyer slipped into a damaged section of the bridge deck, interrupting automotive traffic until dawn. Nevertheless, within 24 hours, the bridgehead on the east bank of the Rhine was packed with almost 8,000 troops including two armored infantry battalions, a tank battalion, a tank destroyer company, nearly three regiments of infantry and almost two anti-aircraft battalions. Many other troops had been ordered to the bridge, with a special emphasis on engineer bridging troops and anti-aircraft battalions.

The first German unit to become aware of the capture of the bridge was the engineer regiment responsible for the bridge, including Maj. August Kraft commander of III./Ld.Pi.Rgt. 12 and his immediate superior, Maj. Herbert Strobel. They both agreed that an immediate counterattack would be necessary, but since Strobel was closer to the bridge, he decided to lead the counterattack while Kraft was dispatched to another threatened bridge near Engers to make sure it was demolished. Strobel gathered about 100 engineers and assorted flak troops as well about a ton of explosives and ordered them towards Remagen about 30km away. In the early hours, Strobel's small force began bumping into the outer perimeter of the American bridgehead and a series of confused exchanges took place in the dark. One of the German groups ran into the newly arrived tanks of the 14th Tank Battalion and their advance was halted and many troops captured. Other German demolition teams bumped into the newly arrived 310th Infantry from the 78th Division and, by dawn, about 100 Germans had been captured. US units continued to police stragglers from the misbegotten attack throughout the morning and the engineers' assault proved to be completely ineffectual.

Model was in transit for most of March 7 and, when his headquarters learned of the capture of the bridge, during the night of March 7–8, the 11th Panzer Division was ordered to move against Remagen without delay. However, the division had only crossed the Rhine on March 6 and was stalled around Düsseldorf because of a lack of fuel. The divisional commander recommended that Panzer Brigade 106 be used instead as it was the only unit ready to move at short notice, but after its battering during the fighting for Bonn, Model wanted a larger unit used at Remagen. The 11th Panzer Division was forced to requisition fuel from local factories, and was unable to begin moving until March 9–10.

The local situation around Remagen was even more confused. Following the failure of Strobel's attack, Gen. Lt. von Berg, commander of Wehrkreis XII Nord formerly in command of all local forces, contacted his headquarters around 0830hrs. He ordered that all remaining engineer units in the area from as far away as Coblenz rally near Hönningen to attack the bridgehead. In the meantime, Gen. Lt. Wirtz, the commander of engineer troops of Army Group B, had already conducted a reconnaissance of the bridgehead and inspected the numerous ferry sites along the Rhine manned by engineer troops assisting in the retreat of Fifteenth Army over the Rhine. When he heard about Berg's orders, he told the engineers to ignore them otherwise the

An M15A1 multiple-gun carriage stands guard over the Rhine on March 17 from a railroad embankment north of Remagen. A few hours later, the Ludendorff Bridge, evident in the background, collapsed. (NARA)

A series of floating barriers were strung across the Rhine by US engineers to prevent the Germans from floating mines down the river against the bridge. (NARA)

ferry operations would collapse. By the end of the day, Model supported Wirtz's decision and the few spare engineer troops still under local command were directed to hold a defensive line near Dattenberg while the other units continued to conduct ferrying operations along the river.

Hitler was enraged to learn of the capture of the bridge on March 8 and the first victim of his tirade was von Rundstedt who was dismissed. Albert Kesselring, who had led German forces in Italy in 1943–45, became the new OB West. Scapegoats were needed to calm Hitler's fury and Model tried to deflect attention from his own role by singling out the hapless Scheller, while other officers likewise indicted junior officers. Summary trials were held for four officers: the erstwhile bridge commander Maj. Scheller, the two engineer officers Kraft and Strobel, and the young Luftwaffe officer Lt. Peters, whose secret rocket battery had crossed the bridge that afternoon. All were convicted and shot, while a fifth officer, Capt. Bratge, was found guilty *in absentia*, having already been captured by the Americans.

CONSOLIDATING THE BRIDGEHEAD

While the US Army was busily reinforcing the Remagen bridgehead, von Zangen's Fifteenth Army was desperately trying to recover the remains of its units from the west bank of the Rhine. Most of the surviving units from 67 Corps had been pushed into a pocket south of Remagen and were being slowly ferried across the river from sites near Brohl and Andernach at night or under cloud cover to avoid Allied fighter-bombers. About 20,000 German troops were captured on the west bank of the Rhine, but a large number made it across the river. The 11th Armored Division assaulted the main southern crossing sites on March 9 and both towns were captured. This attack cleared the main German pocket south of Remagen, capturing 12,555 troops in the process along with much of the corps and divisional artillery. 74 Corps retreated to the river closer to Bonn, but the capture of Bad Godesberg by the 9th Infantry Division in the late afternoon of March 7 sealed off much of this sector

In the meantime, Bayerlein was assigned to create a corps around the remnants of the Panzer Lehr Division, which at this time had only about 15 tanks and 300 men. The 11th Panzer Division was the first reinforcement to arrive in the Remagen area, but a lack of fuel meant that plans for an attack against the bridgehead were continually postponed. Corps Bayerlein also received what was left of the 9th Panzer Division, about 15 tanks and 600 troops, as well as Panzer Brigade 106, which was down to about five tanks after its attempted defense of Bonn. Bayerlein wanted to launch an attack on the bridgehead at dusk on March 10 but Model ordered him to save his forces and start to create a cordon around it. Bayerlein's force later absorbed the staff of the shattered 53 Corps, taking on its name as well. It was assigned the central sector to the immediate east of the bridge as the main defensive element of Fifteenth Army.

The US First Army's delay in exploiting the chaotic state of German defenses was due to debates within the US Army and Eisenhower's SHAEF command about what to do with the Remagen windfall. This debate will be explored in more detail below, but the immediate consequence was to limit the size and mission of the forces in the bridgehead. Nevertheless, the reinforcement of the US bridgehead continued at a steady pace. Both the 9th and 78th Divisions were committed to the bridgehead, with other divisions taking over their previous missions in Operation *Lumberjack*, and they were later reinforced by the 99th Division, with the 7th Armored Division taking up positions on the Rhine. Bradley warned Hodges to limit his advances to about a 1,000m a day until the issue of the eventual mission of the bridgehead could be ironed out. In reality, the advances over the first week of fighting depended in large measure on German resistance and geographic factors, especially the mountainous terrain east of the

ATTACK ON THE LUDENDORFF BRIDGE, MARCH 9, 1945
(pp 54–55)

The Luftwaffe began attacking the Remagen Bridge (1) almost immediately with the first few attacks on March 8. The expectation was that the Stuka would offer the best hope of a pinpoint attack on the bridge, but when all three Stukas were shot down on the first attack mission, it was obvious that another method was needed. German jet strike aircraft seemed a more survivable option since they could outrun Allied fighters and their speed might reduce their vulnerability to the growing anti-aircraft defenses the US Army was deploying around the bridge. At first, Luftwaffe chief Hermann Göring asked for volunteers to fly a suicide mission against the bridge, diving their aircraft directly into the structure. Although there were volunteers, the idea was quickly squashed by senior officers who pointed out that the bomb's safeing and arming system would prevent the bomb from detonating in these circumstances. The second day of Luftwaffe attacks began with an assortment of propeller-driven aircraft including the ubiquitous Fw 190 and Bf 109, but also including the heavy "destroyer" fighters such as the Me 410. The first jet attacks began later that day including both the Me 262 and Arado Ar 234. This shows the attack by 8./KG 76, which staged three sorties that day. The Arado Ar 234 (2) was Germany's first dedicated jet bomber. It had first been deployed in 1944 on a trials basis in the reconnaissance role, but by 1945 the bomber variants were entering service in growing numbers. The first bomber missions by III./KG.76 were conducted in December 1944 over Belgium during the Battle of the Bulge. Although overshadowed by the Me 262 fighter, the Arado was one of the most sophisticated aircraft of its day. It was heavier on take off than the Me 262, so required a rocket-assisted take-off system. The pilot sat in a forward cockpit with excellent forward visibility and a state-of-the-art navigation and bombing system. The usual attack mode was to place the aircraft into a shallow dive at the target, releasing the bomb with the aid of the PV1B periscopic sight tied into the aircraft's BZA bombing computer. As an alternative to dive bombing when attacking area targets from high altitude, the pilot would put the aircraft under autopilot control and then aim at the target using the Lotfe 7K bombsight, which was integrated with the bombing computer to release the bomb automatically at the right moment, but this was not a popular tactic. A third method was the Egon flight-control system which was based around the aircraft's FuG 25a IFF (identification-friend-or-foe) transceiver working in conjunction with two ground-based Freya radars and allowed for blind bombing in the event of cloudy conditions. The jet attacks against Remagen on March 9 proved fruitless, in part due to the intense anti-aircraft fire near the bridge from five US Army anti-aircraft battalions including quad .50-cal. heavy machine guns, 37mm and 40mm automatic cannon, and even 90mm anti-aircraft guns. The aircraft seen here, piloted by Ofw. Friedrich Bruchlos of 8./KG 76, was one of the two jet strike aircraft lost that day when hit by flak.

bridge. The aim was to take a series of phase lines, first to push the bridgehead out beyond small arms range, then push it beyond artillery range and finally to reach and secure the Bonn–Frankfurt autobahn as a springboard for future operations.

German resistance in the first few days after the bridge capture was weak. General Joachim Kortzfleisch, the Wehrkreis III commander, was delegated by Model to command the front until von Zangen's Fifteenth Army could extricate itself from the west bank of the Rhine. He cobbled together some ad hoc formations using *Volkssturm*, Luftwaffe flak units and police units to form a temporary cordon around the bridgehead. The most potent resistance came from German artillery units, which had withdrawn prior to the bridge capture against orders. Unlike the battered infantry, the artillery units still had good morale and set about a deliberate effort to bombard the bridge and bridgehead area. The artillery force at this point included about 50 105mm howitzers, 50 150mm guns and howitzers and about 12 heavy 210mm howitzers. The artillery effort was aided by the hilly terrain, which allowed good observation of the bridgehead in the first few days of the fighting, and at least one artillery observer infiltrated into Remagen with a radio to direct fire. There were repeated direct hits on the Ludendorff Bridge; on March 8–9 alone, the bridge was hit 24 times. On March 10, a gasoline truck on the bridge was hit, forcing a temporary closure and leading the US Army to redirect all gasoline and ammo trucks to river ferries for two days. By March 11, German artillery fire began to diminish in intensity and accuracy; the German forward observer had been discovered, hills overlooking the bridge had been captured, smoke generators masked the bridge and the artillery battalions were running low on ammunition. The Luftwaffe tried to take up the slack.

WONDER WEAPONS VS. THE BRIDGE

Hermann Göring had long been out of Hitler's favor for the continuing collapse of the Luftwaffe, and he attempted to re-enter the Führer's good graces by promising that the Luftwaffe would destroy the bridge. The special squadrons for bridge destruction using the Mistel composite aircraft had already been committed to attack the bridges in the east being used by the Red Army, and bomber units using the Fritz-X guided bomb and Hs.293 missile were inactive because of the lack of fuel and combat losses in 1944. The Luftwaffe in the west was too weak to launch massed attacks on account of the dominating presence of Allied fighters, but the 14th Fliegerdivision under Oberst von Heinemann attempted to stage numerous small-scale attacks with whatever fighters and fighter-bombers could be scraped together. An initial attack was conducted around 1645hrs on March 8 by three Stukas and an Fw 190—all were shot down by the half-tracks of the 482nd AAA Automatic Weapons Battalion, making it clear that dive-bombing was no solution. The only aircraft with a reasonable chance of surviving the Allied air cover were the new jets so Göring ordered the formation of Gefechtsverband Kowalewski, which combined about 30 Me 262A-2a jet fighter-bombers from II./KG 51 and about 40 Ar 234B jet bombers from Obst. Lt. Robert Kowalewski's III./KG 76 into a special combined jet strike force.

One of the few aircraft with a modest chance of surviving the overwhelming Allied air presence around the Remagen Bridge was the Ar 234B2 jet bomber. A single example from KG 76 survives at the Smithsonian National Air and Space Museum's Udvar-Hazy facility in Chantilly, Virginia. (Author)

A pair of 540mm super-heavy mortars of Karl-Batterie 638 was used to bombard the Remagen Bridge, and Karl-Gerät Nr. V "Loki" is seen on its rail transport in April after the US Army captured it. (NARA)

By March 9, there were five US anti-aircraft battalions protecting the bridge, running the gamut from quad .50-cal. machine guns up to 90mm guns. The attacks early in the day included the usual Bf 109 and FW 190 fighters, but also included improvised attacks by Me 410 heavy fighters. The first jet attacks on the bridge began on March 9 and included several Me 262 attacks, as well as three sorties by Ar 234s. One each of the jet types was lost to flak that day, and US units claimed 13 of the 17 German aircraft making attacks. The third day, cloud cover protected the bridge in the morning, but in the afternoon, some 47 attacks were made with the anti-aircraft guns claiming a further 28 aircraft. The danger of low-altitude attacks led to attempts by the Ar 234 bombers to use the advanced Egon blind-bombing system from high altitude on March 12, but this was no more successful. This was the heaviest single day of air attacks involving some 91 aircraft of which the US AA units claimed 26 destroyed and eight damaged. Jet strikes against the bridge peaked on March 13 with 19 Ar 234 sorties out of the 90 sorties flown by the Luftwaffe that day; US AA units claimed 26 shot down and nine damaged. It was also the worst day of the campaign for the Me 262 fighter-bombers, losing five aircraft to flak and Allied fighters. The scale of Luftwaffe attacks dropped dramatically in the next few days because of the losses. By March 13, the anti-aircraft defense reached its peak, with 16 AA gun batteries and 33 automatic weapons batteries for a total of 672 AA weapons around the bridge. Remagen witnessed the densest concentration of US Army anti-aircraft fire anywhere during the war and it accomplished its mission. No German aircraft managed to hit the bridge in the ten days of attacks. Through March 17, the US Army estimated that the Luftwaffe had conducted about 400 sorties against the bridge of which 140 aircraft were claimed to have been shot down and 59 probably destroyed. Gefechtsverband Kowalewski had lost 18 jet aircraft in combat plus several more damaged aircraft crashing on landing, a total of about a third its original strength.

At Himmler's urging, Hitler ordered that the bridgehead area be wiped out using V-2 missiles regardless of civilian losses. Himmler dispatched SS-Abteilung 500, a recently formed missile battalion, to attack the bridgehead. The battalion was armed with an improved version of the V-2 missile with a special radio guidance upgrade, and launched 11 missiles during March 11–17 from bases in the Netherlands without scoring any hits. One missile came within a mile of the bridge, striking inside Remagen; aside from one other hit within the town, the rest of the missiles exploded harmlessly in the river or open countryside. Another special weapon to appear was the Karl 540mm super-heavy mortar. Karl-Batterie

This is one of the frogmen of SS-Jagdverband Südost who attempted to plant explosive charges against the bridges in the Remagen area on the night of March 17. The searchlights on Leaflet CDL tanks stationed along the river foiled the attempt. (NARA)

The first of the tactical bridges across the Rhine near the Ludendorff Bridge was a treadway bridge constructed by the 291st Engineer Combat Battalion completed early on the morning of May 11. (NARA)

A pontoon bridge was constructed south of the Ludendorff Bridge between Kripp on the west bank and Linz by the 51st Engineer Combat Battalion late on March 11. (NARA)

The artillery of Fifteenth Army was one of the few effective weapons available to the Wehrmacht around Remagen. Here a column of GIs advance past a wrecked truck column hit by artillery fire on March 11, 1945. (NARA)

638 with two of these massive weapons was sent to the Remagen area where some 14 rounds were fired starting on March 16; these did not hit the bridge but caused considerable damage within the town of Remagen itself.

There were a number of schemes to float mines down the Rhine to attack the bridge, but the US Army had taken the precaution of setting up floating barriers to shield the bridge. In cooperation with the Kriegsmarine, a special team of frogmen of the SS-Jagdverband Südost was dispatched from Vienna to the Remagen area on March 11 with the aim of swimming to the base of the bridge and emplacing plastic explosive charges. After several postponements, the 11 swimmers set out on the night of March 17, knowing the bridge had fallen earlier in the day, but planning to place explosive charges against the other bridges. The Germans had earlier attempted to destroy the bridge at Nijmegen using frogmen, so there were extensive countermeasures already in place. To prevent nighttime attacks, the 738th Tank Battalion (Special) had been equipped with Leaflet CDL (Canal Defense Light) tanks, a leftover from a failed effort to deploy secret night-fighting tank units. The frogmen soon encountered the countermeasures during the swim, including the practice of dropping grenades periodically in the water from landing craft. Four frogmen were spotted by the Leaflet tanks and captured before they could do any harm, while the rest escaped.

SPANNING THE RHINE

While the US infantry and armored units continued to push the bridgehead east during the first week after the capture, a massive effort was under way in the Remagen–Erpel area to secure the river crossing. Since the bridge was already damaged and continued to suffer significant damage after its capture from German artillery, efforts were made to create a pontoon bridge upstream and a treadway bridge downstream. In the meantime, river crossing was accomplished using Navy LCVP landing craft trucked into the area, as well as Army DUKW amphibious trucks and engineer ferries. The treadway bridge was completed by the 291st Engineer Combat Battalion around dawn on March 11, while the pontoon bridge was completed by the 51st Engineer Combat Battalion by midnight on the same day between Kripp and Linz. The two tactical bridges were more vulnerable to artillery or air attack than the mighty Ludendorff Bridge, but, by March 14, the German air and artillery attacks began tapering off. The two tactical bridges proved vital when around 1500hrs on March 17, the Ludendorff Bridge fell into the Rhine. The US engineers were in the process of repairing the bottom chord of the upstream truss that had been blasted by the demolition charge on March 7 and the delayed effect of this blast was the primary cause of the collapse. The collapse of the rail bridge prompted III Corps to add a floating Bailey bridge to the two other tactical bridges, which opened to traffic around dawn on March 20, 1945.

BLOCKING THE BRIDGEHEAD

On March 10, the new OB West, Field Marshal Kesselring, met with Model and von Zangen to discuss the Remagen situation. By that point, the first elements of the 9th and 11th Panzer Divisions were along the bridgehead fighting against US troops. Three Replacement Army formations, the s.Pz.Jäger.Abt. 512 (Jagdtiger), Pz.Jäger.Abt. 654 (Jagdpanther), and s.Pz.Abt 506 (Kingtiger) were assigned to schwere Panzergruppe Hudel under the command of the skeletal Panzer Lehr Division in the northern sector, but they had still not arrived in the bridgehead area. As a result, the long-delayed attack of 11th Panzer Division against the bridgehead, rescheduled for the morning of March 10, was again delayed by Model. Schwere Panzergruppe Hudel, although nominally the most potent armored force in the area, had little impact in the subsequent fighting. The lack of fuel complicated any efforts to move units into position and the armored vehicles suffered from a high breakdown rate. For example,

Panzergruppe Hudel had little success in stopping the US advance out of the Remagen bridgehead. This Jagdpather tank destroyer of 1./s.Pz.Jg.Abt. 654 was one of three knocked out during the fighting on March 13 near Kaimig-Ginsterhain by an M36 (90mm) tank destroyer. (NARA)

Pz.Jager.Abt. 654, although possessing two dozen Jagdpanther tank destroyers, was seldom able to get much more than a third of its force into the field at any one time. The two companies of clumsy Jagdtiger heavy tank destroyers of s.Pz.Jager.Abt. 512 saw little action until the end of March when they attempted to stop Operation *Voyage*, and a substantial proportion of the 11 vehicles lost was due to mechanical breakdowns.

Von Zangen reported that the infantry elements of 67 and 74 Corps had "hardly any combat value at all" and that the prospects for improvement were grim because of a lack of adequate replacements. Although the Fifteenth Army's order of battle looked impressive on paper, in reality most of the divisions were mere skeletons and could hardly field a regiment of infantry. While the artillery had been the backbone of the German defense up to that point, its abilities were compromised by the almost total lack of fuel that made it impossible to move up ammunition or reposition the guns to avoid the increasingly effective US counter-battery fire. Von Zangen concluded that the best that could be hoped for would be local attacks with limited objectives by Bayerlein's renamed 53 Corps. Von Zangen's assessment was that the US forces would attempt to secure the autobahn as the first stage for an enveloping attack to the northeast. Model disagreed with this assessment, and argued that the US Army would adopt a more cautious approach striking directly north along the Rhine in order to meet up with the US Ninth Army in the Düsseldorf area.

German Army Order of Battle, Rhine Sector, March 10–12, 1945

Fifteenth Army	General der Infanterie Gustav von Zangen
74 Infantry Corps	Gen. der Infanterie Karl Püchler
62nd Volksgrenadier Division	Gen.Maj. Friedrich Kittel
3rd Fallschirmjäger Division	Gen. Maj. Richard Schimpf

An M4A3 (76mm) tank of the 9th Armored Division is seen here in the streets of Leutesdorf on March 22 during efforts to push the bridgehead further south along the Rhine. (NARA)

53 Infantry Corps	Gen. Lt. Fritz Bayerlein
11th Panzer Division	Gen. Lt. Wend von Wietersheim
9th Panzer Division	Oberst Helmut Zollendorf
Schwere Panzergruppe Hudel	Major Helmuth Hudel

67 Infantry Corps	Gen. der Infanterie Otto Hitzfeld
272nd Volksgrenadier Division	Gen. Lt. Eugen König
26th Volksgrenadier Division	Gen. Maj. Heinz Kokott
326th Volksgrenadier Division	Gen. Maj. Erwin Kaschner
89th Infantry Division	Gen. Maj. Richard Bazing
167th Infantry Division	Gen. Lt. Hanskurt Höcker
277th Volksgrenadier Division	Gen. Maj. Wilhelm Viebig
5th Fallschirmjäger Division	Gen. Maj. Ludwig Heilmann

As a result, Model ordered the gradual reorientation of Fifteenth Army to place the most potent forces in the area north of Erpel along the Sieg River to block this expected advance. Reinforcements gradually arrived including the 3rd Panzergrenadier Division, the 340th Volksgrenadier Division, reinforced by Infantry Regiment 130, and another artillery corps. On March 13, a mixed assortment of troops from tank repair depots, Replacement Army personnel and individual tanks scraped up from various locations were hastily formed into an improvised Panzer brigade under Gen. Maj. Von Buttler from the Panzer Lehr Division. Bayerlein hoped to use the new forces to stage a counterattack, but Model refused, realizing that the balance of forces was not in the German favor and that a major counterattack would only weaken an already brittle defense.

The US Army was able to reinforce the bridgehead area much more quickly. On March 13, the 1st Infantry Division from Collins' VII Corps arrived and began a process under which VII Corps would take over control of the northern side of the bridgehead area while III Corps maintained the south. On March 16, the 78th Division captured the first substantial portion of the Ruhr–Frankfurt autobahn, but the progress of the attack was hindered more by the rough terrain than German resistance.

Patton's "Rhine rat race" in mid-March collapsed the German Army Group G defenses in the Saar-Palatinate and opened another route to the Rhine. Here, tanks of the 37th Tank Battalion, 4th Armored Division, reach Alzey, about 10km west of the Rhine, on March 20. (NARA)

On March 18, US units began a broad offensive to push out to the autobahn with the 9th Division reaching the autobahn and the 99th Division reaching the Weid River. By March 20, III Corps had reached the bridgehead line prescribed by Bradley's earlier orders and was awaiting Eisenhower's orders on the future role of First Army in upcoming operations. The American advances, especially the actions by the 1st and 78th Divisions along the northern sector, convinced Model to reinforce this area further. On March 20, the 11th Panzer Division was shifted to 74 Corps. The heavy concentration of armor in the north led Model to shift corps headquarters, with Bayerlein's 53 Corps switching with Püchler's 74 Corps on March 22–23 in anticipation of staging the long-delayed counterattack. Von Zangen opposed this excessive concentration in the northern sector, but to little avail.

NEW STRATEGIC OPTIONS

Prior to the capture of Remagen, Eisenhower's plan had been to concentrate the Allied effort with Montgomery's 21st Army Group and Operation *Plunder*, the main Rhine crossing scheduled for late March. A secondary effort, Operation *Undertone*, was to be conducted by Devers' 6th Army Group in the Saar, which was aimed at finally clearing German forces west of the Rhine and providing a springboard for Patton's Third Army to cross the Rhine near Frankfurt. In addition, Operation *Undertone* was intended to secure the Saar industrial region, which still accounted for about ten percent of German industrial production. The SHAEF staff wanted Bradley to give up more First Army divisions to reinforce Montgomery's Operation *Plunder* and, as a result, the bridgehead was limited to five divisions for the first weeks after the capture. Bradley resisted further weakening First Army by offering Eisenhower a way to exploit Remagen.

Bradley had already studied the possibility of operations in this area in September 1944 when the first debates emerged about the future Allied

Model expected that the breakout from the bridgehead would take place on the northern shoulder and so placed most of his Panzer strength there. This is a Panther Ausf. G of the 11th Panzer Division knocked out during fighting with the 1st Infantry Division near Fernegierscheid during the failed counterattacks that began on March 23. (NARA)

A column from 9th Armored Division passes through Limburg on the Lahn River on March 27. The vehicle to the right is an M7 105mm howitzer motor carriage of the 73rd Armored Field Artillery Battalion. (NARA)

campaign in Germany. Bradley's revised plan, codenamed Operation *Voyage*, recognized that the terrain immediately east of the Remagen bridgehead was too mountainous for mechanized operations. However, the presence of the autobahn nearby presented a real opportunity since it could be used to rapidly move mechanized forces slightly southward towards the Lahn River valley. At this point, First Army could link up with Patton's Third Army and both conduct a parallel right hook aimed at Kassel. In conjunction with Montgomery's Operation *Plunder* further north, this would effectively encircle the Ruhr industrial region, the ultimate operational objective of the late March offensives. While Eisenhower would not immediately commit to Operation *Voyage*, Bradley's proposal convinced him to back away from an unlimited commitment to Montgomery's offensive. When Montgomery again

BOUNCING THE RHINE, MARCH 24–28, 1945

Zuider Zee

HOLLAND

Zwolle

Rheine

North German Plain

Osnabruck

Minden

Weser

Hamelin

XXXXX
H
BLASKOWITZ

XXXX
Twenty-fifth
BLUMENTRITT

Utrecht

Zutphen

Bielefeld

XXXX
First
SCHLEMM

Münster

Paderborn

Lippstadt

Arnhem

Pannerden

Mar 25

Mar 28

Haltern

Lek

IJssel

Waal

XXXX
First   Can
CRERAR

Wesel

Dorsten

Hamm

Lippe

Warburg

Mar 23

Second   Br
DEMPSEY

XXXX

XXXXX
21
MONTGOMERY

Tilburg

Maas

Niers

Roermond

Neuss

Duisburg

Essen

Ruhr

Dortmund

RUHR

Hagen

Brilon

XXXXX
B
MODEL

Kassel

XXXX
Ninth   US
SIMPSON

XXXX
Fifth
HARPE

Düsseldorf

Rhine

Eder

Homberg

Maastricht

Jülich

Roer

Erft

Cologne

XXXX
Fifteenth
ZANGEN

Siegen

GERMANY

Mar 28

Marburg

Aachen

Düren

Bonn

Siegburg

Sieg

Lauterbach

XXXX
First   US
HODGES

Remagen

Mar 7

Rhine

Mar 25

Giessen

BELGIUM

Ourthe

Liege

Meuse

Coblenz

Mar 22

Limburg

Frankfurt

Hanau

Aschaffenburg

Boppard

Mar 25

XXXXX
12
BRADLEY

A r d e n n e s

T h e   E i f e l

Our

Moselle

St Goar

xxx
VIII

Wiesbaden

Mainz

Oppenheim

Darmstadt

Mar 25

LUXEMBOURG

Trier

Bad Kreuznach

XXXX
Third   US
PATTON

Mar 22

Worms

Mar 25

Luxembourg

Mar 26

Mannheim

Eberbach

PALATINATE

Semois

Moselle

Kaiserslautern

Speyer

Heidelberg

SAAR

XXXX
Seventh   US
PATCH

Germersheim

Landau

XXXX
First
FOERTSCH

Heilbronn

Verdun

Meuse

Metz

Saarbrücken

Sarreguemines

Bitche

Wissembourg

Mar 22

Rhine

Karlsruhe

Pforzheim

FRANCE

On March 25, Eisenhower visited III Corps headquarters to discuss the planned Remagen breakout operation. Here, Gen. Hodges (left) explains the operation on a wall map with Gen. van Fleet of III Corps, with Bradley and Eisenhower watching. (NARA)

pressed him with the extravagant demand for another ten US divisions for the already bloated Operation *Plunder*, Eisenhower cleverly conceded the point but on the condition that Bradley's 12th Army Group be given back control of all the US Ninth and First Army units scheduled to participate in *Plunder*. With his bluff called, Montgomery backed off, preferring to have only the US Ninth Army under his control than to have double the US reinforcements but all under Bradley's command.

Eisenhower began to ponder Operation *Voyage* much more seriously because of the success of Operation *Undertone* in the middle of March. This operation was originally conceived as a US Seventh Army campaign to break through the Westwall fortifications in the Saar, a formidable challenge on account of the mountainous terrain and muddy spring weather. Patton was itching to move on the Rhine, and pointed out that the Westwall defenses in the Saar could be outflanked if his Third Army bounced the Moselle River and raced for the Rhine, effectively cutting off the German Army Group G from the rear. Hitler's refusal to countenance any withdrawals from west of the Rhine left the German Army Group G defenses vulnerable. Although many senior US commanders dismissed the promised Moselle offensive as Patton's usual bravado, Bradley saw the merit of the plan and pushed hard for it with Eisenhower. In the pre-dawn hours of March 13, two of Patton's corps began a preliminary bombardment as a prelude to their assault over the Moselle. The ensuing lightning advance into the Saar-Palatinate in the two middle weeks of March was dubbed the "Rhine Rat Race" by the GIs of Third Army after the German units in the area collapsed and began racing back to the Rhine. The German main line of resistance from Trier to Coblenz on the Moselle was pushed all the way back to a line from Mannheim to Mainz on the Rhine, and most of the German Seventh Army was destroyed in the process. It recalled the heady days of August 1944 when Patton's Third Army had raced to Paris. Patch's Seventh Army to the south made excellent progress into the Saar in spite of the Westwall defenses and hilly terrain. Third Army estimated that the opposing German forces had lost 113,000 men in two weeks of fighting including 68,000 prisoners compared with US casualties of 5,220. Seventh Army and attached French units captured 22,000 Germans and estimated that the opposing German formations had lost 75–80 percent of their infantry. As importantly, the advance had placed Third Army within reach of the Rhine, and Patton had already hoarded plenty of tactical bridging for precisely such an opportunity.

The spectacular success of Operation *Undertone* reinforced Eisenhower's preference for a broad front strategy in the endgame against Germany and undermined his commitment to Operation *Plunder* as the sole Allied thrust. The collapse of the Wehrmacht in the Saar-Palatinate was evidence that the German Army was in crisis and could not hold such an extended front. While Montgomery slowly prepared Operation *Plunder*, Army Group G had been shattered and access to central and southern Germany seemed assured. Eisenhower would let *Plunder* proceed, but on March 19, Eisenhower gave Bradley the green light for Operation *Voyage*. First Army was to be prepared to strike for Limburg and the Lahn River valley to link up with Patton. The next phase would depend on the progress of Operation *Plunder*, but once Montgomery was across the Rhine, the US Ninth Army would aim for Kassel to permit an encirclement of the Ruhr industrial region with First Army.

Model initiated his long-delayed counterattack against the Remagen bridgehead on the evening of March 23 using Bayerlein's 53 Corps, starting with an attack by Pz.Gren.Rgt. 111 of the 11th Panzer Division near Eulen Mountain. The attack was intended to push the 11th Panzer Division and schwere Panzergruppe Hudel down the autobahn past the Sieben Mountains into the northern flank of the bridgehead. The attacks were disjointed and piecemeal and easily rebuffed by Collins' VII Corps, which had been given the assignment of holding the northern shoulder while III Corps prepared to start its own offensive on March 25. Prospects for any further attacks were ended on March 24 when Kesselring ordered Model to give up 11th Panzer Division to reinforce the collapsing Army Group G further south.

BREAKOUT FROM REMAGEN: OPERATION *VOYAGE*

Operation *Voyage* was intended to supplement the main Allied Rhine crossing, Operation *Plunder*, which began on March 24. *Plunder* was the most elaborate and lavish Allied operation since the D-Day landings involving the entire British 21st Army Group, reinforced by the US Ninth Army, with a combined force of over a million troops and over 30 divisions, complete with a subordinate airborne landing, Operation *Varsity*. Facing this massive force was the weak Army Group H with barely 85,000 troops and 35 tanks and the northern shoulder of Army Group B, stripped of troops to block the Remagen bridgehead. The Rhine assault began as planned and faced modest resistance.

In contrast to this spectacle, the operations in Bradley's 12th Army Group sector were less celebrated, but ultimately more successful. As a preliminary step to Operation *Voyage*, Bradley authorized Patton's Third Army to cross the Rhine, the first step in a broader right hook to the northwest. Patton wanted to leap the Rhine on the run, and two crossing sites were the most likely. The better of the two was south of Mainz since sites closer to the city involved the crossing of both the Rhine and Main rivers. The Germans recognized this and defenses around Mainz were better prepared. As a result, Patton opted for surprise, and planned the crossing near Oppenheim with a feint at Mainz. On March 22, engineer equipment boats were moved forward to carry the 11th Infantry of the 5th Infantry Division across near Nierstein that night. German defenses along the Rhine in this sector were meager as the German Seventh Army was still retreating over the Rhine after their rout in the Saar-Palatinate. The 11th Infantry set off across the Rhine around 2200hrs, encountering modest German resistance that was quickly overwhelmed. By dawn on March 23, the 5th Infantry Division had two of its regiments across, followed by a third in the morning and a regiment from the 90th Division in the evening. The original engineer contingent swelled with DUKW amphibious truck units, Navy LCVP landing craft and a ferry for tanks, and a 40-ton treadway bridge was erected by afternoon. The Seventh Army attempted to counterattack but could only scrape up an improvised battlegroup from the officer candidate school at Wiesbaden, which was brushed off. To needle his rival Montgomery, Bradley announced the

The initial objective of Operation *Voyage* was the autobahn at Giessen, the hinge point at which the First and Third Armies linked to begin their northward swing to Paderborn. Here, a mechanized column from the 6th Armored Division, Third Army rolls up the autobahn near Giessen on March 29 past a vast number of Wehrmacht prisoners from the shattered 67 Infantry Corps. (NARA)

A Panther Ausf. G tank lies burned out in the streets of Haiger on March 29 after having been knocked out by a tank from the 750th Tank Battalion, supporting the infantry of the 104th Division. The meager Panzer force of Bayerlein's 53 Corps was unable to seriously threaten the advance by the 3rd Armored Division on Paderborn. (NARA)

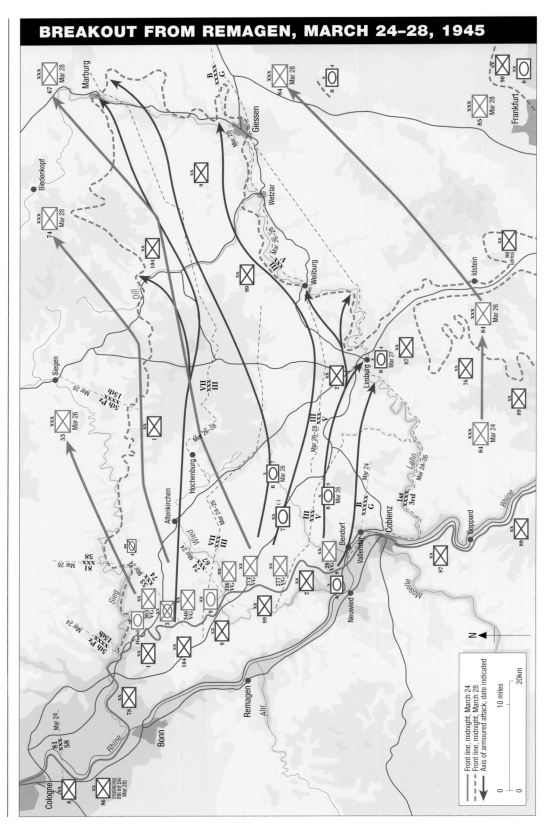

BREAKOUT FROM REMAGEN, MARCH 24–28, 1945

Marburg

Biedenkopf

Giessen

Wetzlar

Frankfurt

Idstein

Weilburg

Dill

Siegen

Limburg

Altenkirchen

Hochenburg

Lahn

Rhine

Boppard

Wied

Coblenz

Moselle

Bendorf

Vallendar

Neuwied

Remagen

Ahr

Bonn

Rhine

Sieg

Hödel

N

Cologne

Front line, midnight, March 24
Front line, midnight, March 28
Axis of armoured attack, date indicated

0   10 miles
0   20km

Schwere Panzergruppe Hudel had little impact on the fighting. This Jagdtiger of 1./s.Pz.Jäger Abt. 512, commanded by Lt. Sepp Tarlach, was abandoned in Obernephen along the Sieg River during the lightning advance by the US 3rd Armored Division. (NARA)

success of the crossing the day before Montgomery's planned operation, pointing out that 12th Army Group could cross the Rhine even without artillery preparation, never mind an airborne assault.

Operation *Voyage* began a day after Operation *Plunder* on March 25, 1945. The pace of the attack was significantly aided by the configuration of German defenses around the Remagen bridgehead. Both Model and von Zangen expected a breakout but Model was convinced that it would come at the northern shoulder to permit First Army to roll up the Rhine and meet up with Ninth Army before pressing an attack against the Ruhr industrial zone. Von Zangen did not think that Bradley would be that cautious, and instead expected that the breakout would originate from the center of the Remagen bridgehead and push to the northeast, encircling the Ruhr. Model had the last word, and Bayerlein's 53 Corps, with the bulk of the Fifteenth Army's operational Panzers, was positioned to resist an expected northern breakout. Von Zangen did receive the concession to leave the next most powerful corps, Püchler's 74 Corps, on a narrow front in the center. The southern bridgehead area was covered by the weakest of the forces, Hitzfeld's 67 Corps, which had an elongated front extending from the Wied River to the northern outskirts of Coblenz, and consisted of beaten-up infantry divisions with little armored support. In fact, the focus of the US First Army attack was in the south, with the aim of seizing and exploiting the autobahn in that area.

Operation *Voyage* started in the pre-dawn hours of March 25 with five infantry and two armored divisions in three corps. Not unexpectedly, the toughest fighting took place in the north opposite Collin's VII Corps with resistance from both the remnants of the Panzer Lehr and 11th Panzer Divisions, which had not yet departed for Army Group G. Nevertheless, the excellent weather permitted extensive close air support from XIX Tactical Air Command, and VII Corps penetrated the German main line of resistance by the early afternoon. Van Fleet's III Corps followed doctrine and led with the infantry, reserving its armor for the second day to start the exploitation phase once the main line of

resistance had been overcome. The 9th Panzer Division was the only source of resistance in the sector, but was so battered that it could impose little delay on the 9th and 99th Divisions, which advanced more than 8km. Gerow's V Corps pushed the 9th Armored Division and 2nd Infantry Division to the southeast with the aim of linking up with Patton's Third Army near Limburg along the Lahn River, crunching through the weak 67 Corps front with little difficulty.

By March 26, it was becoming evident that the German defenses were disintegrating. The 4th Armored Division from Patton's Third Army had broken out of the Oppenheim bridgehead to the south, had cleared the Main River, and was heading north for the link-up. Collins' VII Corps was making excellent progress in spite of a limited counterattack by the Panzer Lehr Division. The Fifteenth Army had 40 Panzers in repair in a depot in Altenkirchen, and these were lost when 3rd Armored Division enveloped the town, a major setback for an army short of mobile firepower. III Corps passed the 7th Armored Division through its infantry divisions and it set off on a race for the intermediate objective, the town of Giessen that was intended as the hinge for the northward strike behind the Ruhr industrial region. General Püchler's 74 Corps had been completely routed and posed little resistance. General Höhne's 84 Corps became trapped between the US First and Third Armies, and its collapse in the face of the sequential attacks left a gaping hole between Army Group B and Army Group G. Von Zangen's Fifteenth Army headquarters had lost touch with all three of its corps, and only Bayerlein's 53 Corps had much substance by the end of March 26. Model contacted Bayerlein directly and ordered him to relinquish the defense of the Sieg River line to the Fifth Panzer Army and concentrate instead on a counterattack

While the First Army was breaking out of the Remagen bridgehead, Patton's Third Army to the south was crossing the Rhine. Here, troops of the 89th Division huddle inside a DUKW amphibious truck as they come under small-arms fire while crossing the Rhine on March 26. (NARA)

across the three US corps to Limburg. Bayerlein later called the order, "impossible, entirely hopeless, and insane."

The northern arm of the Ruhr encirclement was the US Ninth Army, still a part of Montgomery's Operation *Plunder*. The heavily reinforced XVI Corps conducted the US Army portion of the attack, dubbed Operation *Flashpoint*, in the pre-dawn hours of March 25. As in the British and Canadian sectors, the Rhine crossing proceeded with little difficulty. However, further progress in this sector was hampered by the congested bridgehead sector, diversion of Ninth Army bridges to British units and resistance from the 116th Panzer Division. By March 28, these problems had largely been overcome when the US 513th Parachute Infantry mounted on Churchill tanks of the British 6th Guards Brigade outflanked the 116th Panzer Division and much of the rest of 47 Panzer Corps, while at the same time, Montgomery freed up the Wesel bridges for the Ninth Army's use. The way was now open for a northern encirclement of the Ruhr.

By March 28, the progress opposite the Remagen bridgehead had been so impressive that Bradley began refining the movements of Operation *Voyage*. Hodges' First Army was directed to begin the swing northward, with the objective being Paderborn, while Patton's Third Army would take the right flank and advance alongside to the northeast, aiming at Kassel. The spearhead of the First Army advance was Collins' VII Corps with the lead taken by the 3rd Armored Division reinforced by the 414th Infantry Regiment from the 104th Division. Each combat

An armored reconnaissance unit of the 3rd Armored Division led by an M5A1 light tank passes through a German town south of Paderborn on March 29. (NARA)

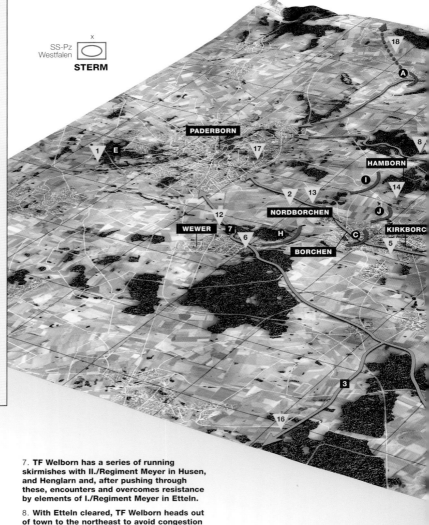

US UNITS

3rd Armored Division
(Maj. Gen. Maurice Rose)

1 83rd Armored Reconnaissance Battalion

Combat Command A (Brig. Gen. Doyle Hickey)

2 Task Force* Doan/Boles (Col. Leander
Doan/Lt. Col. John Boles)

3 Task Force Kane (Lt. Col. Matthew Kane)
32nd Armored Rgt. (-3rd Bn.)
1/36th Armored Infantry Rgt.
1/414th Infantry Rgt.
A/23rd Armored Engineer Bn.
A/703rd Tank Destroyer Bn.
67th Armored Field Artillery Bn.
83rd Armored Field Artillery Bn.

Combat Command B
(Brig. Gen. Truman Boudinot)

4 Task Force Lovelady
(Lt. Col. William Lovelady)

5 Task Force Welborn (Col. John Wellborn)
33rd Armored Rgt. (-3rd Bn.)
2/26th Armored Infantry Rgt.
2/414th Infantry Rgt.
B/703rd Tank Destroyer Bn.
B/23rd Armored Engineer Bn.
391st Armored Field Artillery Bn.

Combat Command R (Col. Robert Howze)

6 Task Force Richardson
(Lt. Col. Walter Richardson)

7 Task Force Hogan (Lt. Col. Samuel Hogan)
3/32nd Armored Rgt.
3/33rd Armored Rgt.
3/36th Armored Infantry Rgt.
3/414th Infantry Rgt.
C/703rd Tank Destroyer Bn.
C/23rd Armored Engineer Bn.
54th Armored Field Artillery Bn.

(*task force attachments varied from day to day from Combat
Command units)

▼ EVENTS

**1. SS-Ersatz Panzer Brigade Westfalen
is formed on the afternoon of March 29
from training staff and other personnel
at the Sennelager training grounds north
of Paderborn.**

**2. SS-Ersatz Panzer Brigade Westaflen
deploys in an arc south of Paderborn on
evening of March 29, Regiment Meyer to
the west of the Paderborn–Kirchbochen
road and Regiment Holzer to the east.**

**3. 3rd Armored Division reconnaissance
elements from the 83rd Armored
Reconnaissance Battalion run into German
defenses from the 1st Battalion, Regiment
Meyer, at Wünnenberg early on March 30,
and allow TF Richardson to pass through.**

**4. 3rd Armored Division reconnaissance
elements from the 83rd Armored
Reconnaissance Battalion run into German
defenses from the 2nd Battalion, Regiment
Meyer, at Husen early on March 30, and allow
TF Welborn to pass through.**

**5. TF Richardson pushes through Wünnenberg
and Haaren during the morning, but becomes
engaged in heavy fighting with I./Regiment
Meyer in "bazooka town"—Kirchbochen.**

**6. TF Hogan skirts past light defenses on the
westernmost route, but finally encounters
stiffer resistance from I./Regiment Meyer in
Wewer where a firefight continues through
most of March 30.**

**7. TF Welborn has a series of running
skirmishes with II./Regiment Meyer in Husen,
and Henglarn and, after pushing through
these, encounters and overcomes resistance
by elements of I./Regiment Meyer in Etteln.**

**8. With Etteln cleared, TF Welborn heads out
of town to the northeast to avoid congestion
along the Kirchborchen route being used by
TF Richardson.**

**9. In late afternoon, Kingtiger tanks of
2./s.Pz.Abt. 507 move out of woods near
Hamborn and cut behind TF Welborn, shooting
up the rear columns.**

**10. TF Doan following behind TF Welborn is
ordered to move forward to deal with German
tank threat.**

**11. While attempting to move between the
task forces, the jeep of divisional commander,
Maj. Gen. Maurice Rose, is trapped by
Kingtiger tanks and Rose is killed around
dusk while trying to surrender.**

**12. TF Hogan secures Wewer on March 31
and prepares to move into Paderborn the
following day.**

**13. Using flamethrowers to overcome
stubborn resistance, TF Richardson fights
its way through "bazooka town" and clears
Kirchborchen, Borchen, and Nordborchen
on March 31.**

**14. Most of s.Pz.Abt. 507 withdraws on March
31 but a force of five Kingtiger tanks and 200
infantry attack TF Boles near Hamborn but are
beaten back.**

**15. 83rd Reconaissance Battalion seizes
Dörenhagen and Eggeringhausen, and is
relieved later in the day by TF Lovelady, which
has finally freed itself from a prolonged battle
with Infantry Replacement Battalion 194 in
Wrexen.**

**16. TF Kane dispatched before dawn on
Easter Sunday, April 1, to link up with 2nd
Armored Division 20 miles to the west at
Lippstadt, closing the Ruhr encirclement;
US forces meet around 1530hrs.**

**17. Four taskforces (Hogan, Richardson,
Welborn, Lovelady) fight their way into
Paderborn on April 1; the city is cleared
by 1700hrs.**

**18. The remnants of SS-Ersatz Panzer Brigade
Westfalen retreat eastward to link up with the
Eleventh Army in the Harz Mountains.**

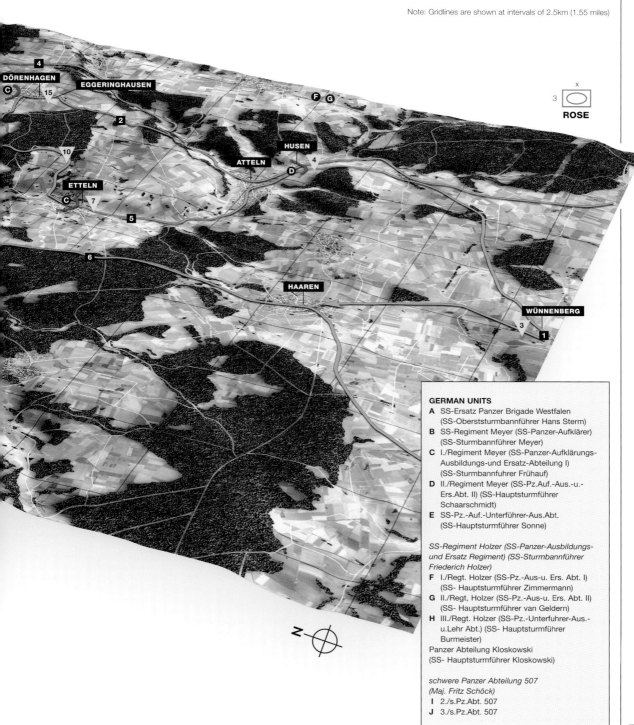

The battle for Paderborn

Note: Gridlines are shown at intervals of 2.5km (1.55 miles)

DÖRENHAGEN

EGGERINGHAUSEN

ROSE

HUSEN

ATTELN

ETTELN

HAAREN

WÜNNENBERG

GERMAN UNITS

A SS-Ersatz Panzer Brigade Westfalen
(SS-Oberststurmbannführer Hans Sterm)

B SS-Regiment Meyer (SS-Panzer-Aufklärer)
(SS-Sturmbannführer Meyer)

C I./Regiment Meyer (SS-Panzer-Aufklärungs-
Ausbildungs-und Ersatz-Abteilung I)
(SS-Sturmbannfuhrer Frühauf)

D II./Regiment Meyer (SS-Pz.Auf.-Aus.-u.-
Ers.Abt. II) (SS-Hauptsturmführer
Schaarschmidt)

E SS-Pz.-Auf.-Unterführer-Aus.Abt.
(SS-Hauptsturmführer Sonne)

*SS-Regiment Holzer (SS-Panzer-Ausbildungs-
und Ersatz Regiment) (SS-Sturmbannführer
Friederich Holzer)*

F I./Regt. Holzer (SS-Pz.-Aus-u. Ers. Abt. I)
(SS- Hauptsturmführer Zimmermann)

G II./Regt, Holzer (SS-Pz.-Aus-u. Ers. Abt. II)
(SS- Hauptsturmführer van Geldern)

H III./Regt. Holzer (SS-Pz.-Unterfuhrer-Aus.-
u.Lehr Abt.) (SS- Hauptsturmführer
Burmeister)
Panzer Abteilung Kloskowski
(SS- Hauptsturmführer Kloskowski)

*schwere Panzer Abteilung 507
(Maj. Fritz Schöck)*

I 2./s.Pz.Abt. 507

J 3./s.Pz.Abt. 507

During the confused fighting south of Paderborn on March 30, Maj. Gen. Maurice Rose, commander of the 3rd Armored Division, was killed after a column of Kingtiger tanks of s.Pz.Abt. 507 trapped his jeep. He was the only US armored division commander killed in combat in World War II. (NARA)

command of the 3rd Armored Division was allotted additional infantry battalions, and the remaining infantry elements of the 104th Division were motorized using any trucks available to create a mobile infantry follow-on force. On March 29, the armored column raced over 70km, with Combat Command B ending up about 25km south of Paderborn by midnight. Casualties had been light and no significant German resistance was encountered.

THE BATTLE FOR PADERBORN

The collapse of the Fifteenth Army along the Remagen bridgehead proved far more worrisome to Model than the massive Rhine crossing by 21st Army Group around Wesel as the rapid collapse of the defenses around the bridgehead was completely unanticipated and the direction of the US attack was potentially disastrous. With US armored columns racing deep behind Fifteenth Army, the risk of an encirclement of the whole of Army Group B was an alarming possibility. Model attempted to prevent an encirclement by activating a new corps in the Harz Mountains east of the Ruhr, and by reorienting Bayerlein's 53 Corps for yet another hopeless mission, this time to strike the US armored spearhead on its left flank as it advanced northward. Model also activated a new formation on the afternoon of March 29, SS-Panzer-Ersatz Brigade Westfalen, using troops from the Waffen-SS Panzer and Panzer reconnaissance schools at Sennelager, north of Paderborn. The brigade was commanded by Oberststurmbannführer Hans Stern and consisted of two improvised infantry regiments raised from the training staff and students, with a single tank company using 15 old training tanks such as PzKpfw IIIs. Besides the Waffen-SS cadre troops, Sennelager was also the location for

3./s.Pz.Jg.Abt. 512 from schwere Panzergruppe Hudel arrived in the final phase of the fighting for Paderborn and one of their massive Jagdtiger 128mm tank destroyers was lost there during the fighting with the 3rd Armored Division on April 1, 1945. (MHI)

re-equipping army tank battalions with the new Kingtiger heavy tank, which was manufactured in nearby Kassel. As a result, the brigade received s.Pz.Abt. 507 as its main Panzer component. This was an experienced Tiger battalion that was at Sennelager to replenish after its heavy losses on the Eastern Front. At the end of March, it had 21 Kingtigers and three Jagdpanthers on hand. The hastily improvised brigade deployed south of Paderborn in the early morning hours of Good Friday, March 30. SS-Regiment Meyer covered the main approaches to Paderborn to the south while SS-Regiment Holzer moved down the road towards Lichtenau, intending to create a defensive line along the Diemel River at Scherfede. The deployment was done in haste and left a badly exposed western flank.

The 3rd Armored Division was deployed in its usual configuration with two of its three combat commands forward and one in reserve, in this case CCR on the left and CCB on the right, with CCA following behind. Each of the combat commands was broken into two task forces, each based around a mixture of tank and infantry companies with other supporting units attached. The usual battle deployment was to approach the objective along four routes, with each task force taking one route. In the vanguard was the 83rd Armored Reconnaissance Battalion under divisional control. The recon troops were the first to encounter Panzer Brigade Westfalen in the early morning hours of March 30 in the villages of Husen and Wünneberg. The recon troops were designed for scouting, not close combat, so they stepped aside and let the following task forces pass through to conduct the assault.

Task Force (TF) Richardson pushed through a company of SS-Rgt. Meyer at Wünneberg and then encountered a battalion holding the string of towns and villages around Borchen in Paderborn's southern suburb. The area was soon dubbed "bazooka town" as the Waffen-SS

THE DEVIL IS LOOSE ON THE PADERBORN ROAD, NIGHTFALL, MARCH 30, 1945 (pp 78–79)

On March 30, the third company of schwere Panzer Abteilung 507 (3./s.Pz.Abt.507) under the command of Hptm. Wolf Kolterman, was deployed in the woods immediately south of Paderborn while the second company was deployed further to the southeast. The company was ordered to provide support to SS-Regiment Meyer from SS-Panzer Brigade Westfalen, but saw very little combat during the day as Combat Command B, 3rd Armored Division, methodically fought its way northward through the roadblocks and villages south of the city. The battalion had arrived at the Sennelager military camp in mid-February 1945 to re-equip with the new Kingtiger heavy tanks after a harrowing campaign on the Eastern Front trying to hold back the Soviet winter offensive. The battalion was credited with the destruction of more than 600 Soviet tanks and had six Knight's Cross holders in its ranks, including Kolterman who received his on March 11. By the end of March, only two of the companies had received their new tanks, including 21 Kingtigers and three Jagdpanther tank destroyers. By late afternoon on Good Friday, March 30, TF Welborn had fought its way north through several German villages defended by the infantry of SS-Panzer Brigade Westfalen. Around dusk, its lead column finally reached the woods beyond Etteln and turned west along the road towards Borchen, hoping to connect to a minor back road into Paderborn. The column consisted of two companies of M4 medium tanks intermixed with two companies of armored infantry in M3 half-tracks. Near the head of the column was Col. John Welborn, commander of the 33rd Armored Regiment, riding in a jeep. Towards the rear of the column was the divisional commander, Gen. Rose, hoping to be with the lead team entering Paderborn that night. Around 1530hrs, the column came under long-range fire from Kingtiger heavy tanks (1) of the third platoon, 3./s.Pz.Abt. 507, hidden in a tree line on the high ground overlooking the road about a 1,000m away. The American column halted and radioed for air support. Around 1600hrs, a formation of P-47 Thunderbolts screamed over the tree line and dropped a string of 250kg bombs. Assuming that the German tanks had been neutralized, around twilight the column moved out again and swung on a small road northward towards Hamborn Castle. In the gathering dark, the US column was hit along its length from two concealed Kingtiger platoons. After shooting up the column, Kolterman requested permission from the battalion to finish the job and, around 1930hrs, both platoons moved forward and began to attack the surviving vehicles along the road. Kolterman later recalled that "the Devil was loose on the road." It was during this final action that Gen. Rose's jeep was trapped while trying to escape, and the general killed. TF Welborn suffered heavy losses that evening including 17 M4 tanks, 17 half-tracks and numerous tactical vehicles; 3./s.Pz.Abt. 507 lost no tanks that evening, but lost three Kingtiger tanks the next day to a US ambush.

troops tried to stop the mechanized column mainly with Panzerfaust anti-tank rocket launchers. Kirchborchen, the southernmost portion of the area, was attacked in the early afternoon by Co. G, 36th Armored Infantry, with tank support, which cleared the village and proceeded into the heart of Borchen. The neighboring formation from CCR, TF Hogan, proceeded most of the way to Paderborn against little resistance but finally encountered the outer defenses of the city in the town of Wewer where it spent most of the day fighting with SS cadets.

The two eastern task forces from CCB ran into the center of the German defenses. The easternmost formation, TF Lovelady, encountered most of SS-Rgt. Holzer in Scherfede and spent the entire day trying to fight its way through the town. TF Welborn passed through the recon troops in the early morning at Husen and ran a gauntlet of small road-blocks and defenses in the villages of Atteln, Henglarn and Etteln. It appeared that TF Welborn had cracked the center of the defenses after passing out of Etteln and so the divisional commander, Gen. Maurice Rose, following closely in his jeep, ordered TF Doan from the reserve CCA to reinforce the attack. However, a Kingtiger company was stationed around Hamborn to the west of the breakthrough and at twilight staged a counterattack that managed to cut off the forward column of TF Welborn from TF Doan. After shooting up the trapped column from their ambush positions, the Kingtiger platoons emerged from the woods around dark to overrun the remnants of the column. General. Rose attempted to escape but, while passing one of the tanks, the jeep was pinned and Rose and his driver were captured. In the confusion of the fighting, the tank commander barked instructions to Rose in German, and, thinking he was being instructed to disarm, Rose reached for his pistol belt. The nervous German tanker thought the motion was hostile, and shot and killed Rose.

The vicious fighting in the southern outskirts of Paderborn continued through March 31, with the German infantry defending tenaciously. After suffering heavy casualties from German infantry armed with Panzerfaust anti-tank rockets ensconced in buildings and ruins, TF Richardson brought up flamethrowers. A Kingtiger platoon again attempted to counterattack near Hamborn, but this time lost three tanks to an ambush. Although it was not clear at the time, the day's fighting had largely broken the back of the SS-Panzer Brigade Westfalen's defense. TF Hogan was clear of Wewer and ready to move into the city. TF Richardson was finally clear of Borchen and fought its way through Nordborchen. TF Doan, now renamed TF Boles after the command changes in the wake of Rose's death, had cleared the Hamborn area of the Kingtiger company and its associated infantry. SS-Regt. Holzer was retreating eastward after being pushed out of the way by TF Lovelady, which finally arrived near Dörenhagen to take up the right flank of the final assault on Paderborn.

While SS-Panzer Brigade Westfalen was assigned to blunt the spearhead of the US First Army at Paderborn, Model had ordered a more extensive attack to entirely cut off the spearhead and ensure that the Ruhr was not encircled. The western wing of this attack was Bayerlein's badly overused and under-equipped 53 Corps, while the eastern element was supposed to be a corps-sized formation forming at Kassel. In fact, the eastern force was largely illusory, as the German 166th Infantry Division, freshly arrived from Denmark, had already been

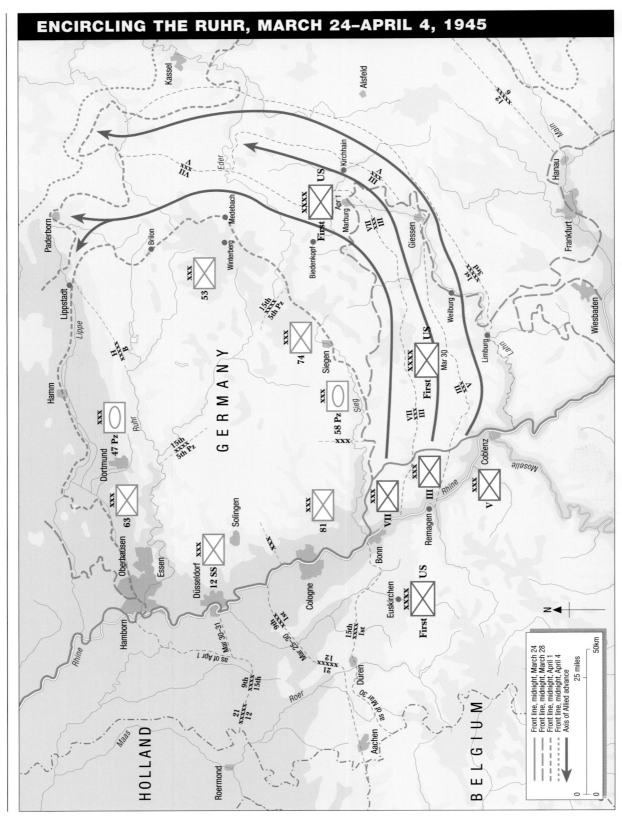

82

On April 16, the staff of the German 53 Corps, headed by Gen. Lt. Fritz Bayerlein, surrendered to Maj. Gen. Robert Hasbrouck of the 7th Armored Division at his mobile command post near Menden, Germany. (NARA)

decimated in fighting against US III Corps days earlier. 53 Corps attack began from the Winterberg area on the night of March 30, consisting of two *Kampfgruppen* of infantry and pioneers supported by 12 Panzers, a few assault guns but no artillery. Instead of cutting behind the rear of the 3rd Armored Division as expected, the German units ran into elements of the 104th Division, which had advanced unexpectedly fast by using every available truck to create an improvised motorized infantry task force. As a result, the desperate counterattack fizzled out as a mere nuisance raid, tying down the 415th Infantry Regiment for a day. Bayerlein's 53 Corps would attempt to stage other attacks over the next few days, but with no more success. By this stage, Allied intelligence had decrypted German message traffic and the German plans and problems were well understood, and readily countered.

ENCIRCLING THE RUHR

The fighting around Paderborn was taking Collins' VII Corps longer than expected to clear, leaving a path open for a German retreat to the north of Paderborn. Ignoring the usual channels, late on March 31 Collins phoned directly to Lt. Gen. William Simpson, the commander of the Ninth Army, about the scheduled link-up. By this stage, Operation *Flashpoint* was proceeding beyond expectations, already having crashed through the German 1st Parachute Army and cut off Army Group H from Army Group B. Collins asked Simpson to detach a combat command from the 2nd Armored Division to advance towards Lippstadt to ensure a timely encirclement of the Ruhr. Shortly after midnight on Easter Sunday, April 1, CCB of the 2nd Armored Division sent one of its task forces towards Lippstadt while, shortly before dawn, TF Kane from the 3rd Armored Division set out for Lippstadt from the opposite direction. Resistance to the eastern advance came mainly from Luftwaffe flak units, which were quickly overrun. By 1530hrs, the two US task forces made first contact near Lippstadt encircling the Ruhr pocket.

The fighting around Paderborn on Easter Sunday was largely anti-climactic after the intense fighting of the previous two days. The surviving elements of SS-Panzer Brigade Westfalen had already begun to withdraw eastward to link up with German forces in the Harz Mountains. The defense was not well organized, consisting of small detachments with little central control. The city had been reduced to rubble by an air attack by 250 RAF Lancaster bombers on March 27, which had unleashed 1,200 tons of bombs. Paderborn was assaulted by four task forces and was finally occupied by 1700hrs. From the start of Operation *Voyage* a week earlier until April 1, the 3rd Armored Division had captured 20,200 prisoners, destroyed or captured 66 tanks and assault guns, 50 artillery pieces, 49 anti-

German troops surrender to the US 99th Division during the concluding phase of the Ruhr encirclement. The vehicle in the foreground is a Volkswagen Schwimmwagen amphibious vehicle. (MHI)

tank guns, 146 flak guns and over 1,250 vehicles. Its own losses during the week of Operation *Voyage* had been 125 killed and 504 wounded as well as 42 M4 medium tanks 11 M5A1 light tanks and 19 half-tracks, most of the casualties taking place in the ferocious fighting around Paderborn.

The strategic objective of Operation *Voyage* was to encircle the Ruhr in order to cut off its military industries. Although it was assumed that a significant number of German troops would be encircled, the expectation was that only about 70,000 troops would be left in the pocket. Bradley had not counted on Hitler's stand-fast orders and had expected that many units would retreat eastward. In fact, the pocket contained about 370,000 German troops, most of the remains of the entire Army Group B. Model had hoped to withdraw the main elements of Army Group B from the Ruhr starting on March 29 in order to continue the fight from more tenable positions in central Germany, especially the Harz Mountains. However, on March 28, Hitler had announced that the Ruhr industrial region was now designated as *Festung Ruhr*, and therefore there would be no retreat; Army Group B would fight or die. Hitler expected that Army Group B could last for months using the industrial resources in the Ruhr; Model radioed Berlin that supplies would last only two to three weeks. Because of the large number of support units and Luftwaffe personnel, only 20 percent of his troops had infantry weapons, another 20 percent had only pistols. Requests for airlift of supplies was denied knowing full well that any such attempt would evaporate in the face of overwhelming Allied airpower.

THE ENDGAME

On the evening of March 28, command of the US Ninth Army reverted from Montgomery's 21st Army Group to Bradley's 12th Army Group to provide a unified command for the reduction of the Ruhr Pocket. With the link-up of the US First and Ninth Armies at Lippstadt on Easter Sunday, the primary focus of Bradley's 12th Army Group after Operation *Voyage* was eastward towards the Elbe River to link up with the Red Army. The secondary mission was the reduction of the Ruhr Pocket. A new army, the Fifteenth, was brought up for occupation duty and held a line along the Rhine, while both the US Ninth and First Armies left behind two corps each to gradually reduce and mop up the Ruhr pocket. There was significant fighting during the first two weeks of the encirclement, but German units were quickly running out of ammunition and news of the Soviet advance on Berlin and the US Army race to the Elbe made it clear to the encircled troops that the end was near. During the first two weeks of April, most US divisions surrounding the Ruhr were capturing about 500 German prisoners a day but by April 14 there was a dramatic change and the daily totals were often 2,000 or more by each division. Army Group B was rapidly disintegrating. Model's chief of staff, Gen. Maj. Karl Wagener, had urged Model to negotiate a surrender on April 7, but Model knew that Hitler would refuse. By mid-April, with the situation hopeless, Model decided to dissolve Army Group B rather than to surrender it. The many underage and overage troops were simply discharged from the army on April 15, and all non-combatant troops were allowed to surrender on April 17. In fact, the remaining pockets were

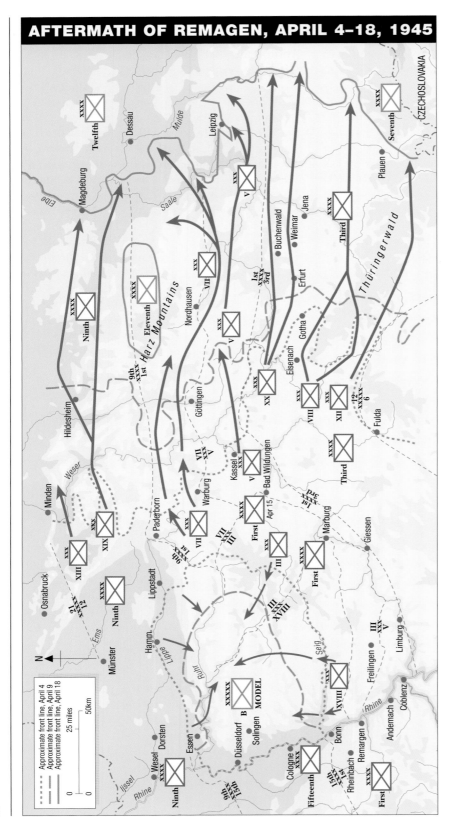

AFTERMATH OF REMAGEN, APRIL 4–18, 1945

Following the encirclement of Model's Army Group B in the Ruhr pocket in early April, the Wehrmacht was unable to erect cohesive defensive lines in central and southern Germany. The Harz Mountains served as a staging area for an unsuccessful effort to create a new Eleventh Army but it was enveloped by the US Ninth Army to the north and the First Army to the south before it became a significant threat. The strategic focus of the US Army campaign in mid-April 1945 was to exploit the collapse of the Wehrmacht by advancing rapidly to the Elbe River to meet Soviet forces, while at the same time reducing and eliminating the Ruhr Pocket using follow-on forces such as the newly arrived Fifteenth Army.

CZECHOSLOVAKIA

Twelfth
Dessau
Mulde
Leipzig
Magdeburg
Saale
Elbe
Seventh
Plauen
Ninth
Harz Mountains
Nordhausen
Buchenwald
Jena
Weimar
Third
Thüringerwald
Erfurt
Eleventh
9th XXXX 1st
Göttingen
Eisenach
Gotha
VII
V
VIII
XII
Fulda
Hildesheim
Kassel
Warburg
Bad Wildungen
Third
Minden
Weser
XIX
Paderborn
First
Apr 15
Marburg
Giessen
XIII
Lippstadt
First
Osnabrück
Ninth
Hamm
MODEL B
Freilingen
Limburg
Münster
Lippe
Ruhr
Seig
Ems
Ijssel
Rhine
Dorsten
Düsseldorf
Solingen
Rhine
Coblenz
Wesel
Ninth
Cologne
Bonn
Andernach
Rheinbach
Remagen
Fifteenth
First

N

Approximate front line, April 4
Approximate front line, April 9
Approximate front line, April 18

0   25 miles
0   50km

disintegrating, with or without orders. Von Zangen and the remaining staff of the Fifteenth Army surrendered on April 13 and Panzer Lehr Division on April 15. By April 18 the pocket had largely collapsed. In total, some 317,000 German troops surrendered in the Ruhr, a greater total than even Stalingrad or Tunisia. Model told his staff that "a field marshal does not surrender," and on April 21 he went alone into the woods and shot himself.

The destruction of Army Group B in the Ruhr pocket marked the end of large-scale operations by the Wehrmacht in the west, leading to what Kesselring called the "makeshift campaign"—a disjointed effort to conduct local defensive actions by the few divisions that had sufficient morale to continue the fight under such hopeless circumstances. The war would go on for another few weeks, but the outcome by now was obvious.

AFTERMATH

The capture of the bridge at Remagen precipitated a major change in the Allied conduct of the final campaign against Germany. Ever since September 1944, it had been the cornerstone of Allied plans that Montgomery's 21st Army Group would be the vanguard of the Allied push into the Ruhr, first with Operation *Market-Garden* and later with Operation *Plunder*. Early in March 1945, Eisenhower continued to expect the focus of Allied operations to be in the north with Montgomery's Operation *Plunder*, which would lead to a deep envelopment of Army Group B in conjunction with the smaller Operation *Undertone* on the lower Rhine. When Simpson offered to make an impromptu leap over the Rhine with the US Ninth Army in early March, Eisenhower deferred to "the Plan." Remagen upset this conception of the endgame against Germany since it permitted a quicker and shallower envelopment of Army Group B.

After the grueling winter fighting of 1944–45, it took some time for the senior Allied commanders to realize that the Wehrmacht was in a very deep crisis. The Allied campaign to reach the Rhine in February and March 1945 had cost the Wehrmacht about 400,000 casualties, including 280,000 prisoners. Besides these tangible losses, there was a palpable collapse in German morale and discipline as more and more officers and soldiers reached the conclusion that defeat was imminent. Hitler's stand-fast orders had made a bad situation even worse by depriving otherwise skilled commanders like Model, von Zangen and Kesselring of the tactical flexibility needed in the conduct of their operations. Shackled to the

The encirclement of Army Group B in the Ruhr enabled the US army to race into central and southern Germany. Many infantry units used their attached tank and tank destroyer battalions to form mobile task forces to speed the advance like this squad from the 328th Infantry, 26th Division riding an M4A3 (76mm) tank of the 778th Tank Battalion on April 29 while moving on the Ilz River. (NARA)

Infantry of the 30th Division fight their way into Braunschweig (Brunswick) on April 10, 1945, with the support of an M4A3E8 tank of the 743rd Tank Battalion. (NARA)

Westwall by Hitler's orders, Army Group B suffered irreparable damage in March 1945.

Eisenhower's strategic changes in the last two weeks of March were prompted by several related factors. The elephantine extravaganza of Operation *Plunder* was a reminder of Montgomery's cautious and laborious tactical style. While this approach might have been prudent when the Wehrmacht was at its prime, it was excessively timid when the Wehrmacht was disintegrating. The contrast with Bradley's 12th Army Group was striking; Patton's aggressive Saar-Palatinate campaign helped to undermine Army Group G and Bradley was promising much the same fate for Army Group B with Operation *Voyage*. Eisenhower recognized that the US Army commanders had adapted to the opportunities presented by the crisis in the Wehrmacht. They were advocating and carrying out bold operations that exploited the brittle German defenses while Montgomery was slow to adapt. Instead of the British 21st Army Group conducting the Ruhr encirclement, the task went instead to the US 12th Army Group.

Beyond the Ruhr encirclement, Eisenhower also was obliged to decide how to conduct the final campaign against Germany. Montgomery and the British Chiefs of Staff continued to push for a northern focus in the final campaign in Germany, and still held hopes for an assault towards Berlin. This was unlikely for several reasons, both tactical and strategic. From the tactical standpoint, the February–March 1945 fighting had validated Eisenhower's broad front tactics. Montgomery's monotonous insistence on a single thrust had come to sound more like self-centered pleading than a desirable strategic approach. The Wehrmacht in the west did not have the resources to deal with a broad front advance so the consequences of minor mistakes such as Remagen were magnified. The critical US successes including the race through the Saar-Palatinate, and the breakout from the Remagen bridgehead were both made possible by the exceptionally brittle German defenses and the lack of mobile reserves. The broad front tactics exploited Allied advantages in combat power and prevented the Wehrmacht from concentrating its very emaciated forces against a narrow front.

Berlin was an unlikely objective for many reasons. Roosevelt, Churchill and Stalin had already accepted that Berlin would be within the Soviet zone of occupation; at the beginning of April the Red Army was only 65km from Berlin at the time compared to the 300–500km of the 21st Army Group. Given his command style, the idea that Montgomery could execute a lightning strike towards Berlin was more than a little preposterous. The capture of Berlin was a matter of political prestige, but held less attraction for Eisenhower than for Montgomery and Churchill. Eisenhower had Gen. George Marshall's confidence and by default, that of the president. In addition, Eisenhower was becoming concerned about reports of the German build-up of an "Alpine redoubt" in Bavaria in southern Germany as a remaining center for last-ditch defense. Eisenhower wanted the war ended as expeditiously as possible, and the most plausible avenue to end German resistance was to exploit the Allied momentum and the German disintegration with a vigorous advance on all fronts, preventing the Nazi diehards from creating pockets of resistance in remote areas. The capture of the bridge at Remagen hastened the end of the war in the west.

THE BATTLEFIELD TODAY

The Remagen Bridge no longer exists. After it fell on March 17, 1945, US engineers began the gradual task of clearing the debris. The last of the steel structures were cleared after the war, but the two stone piers remained in the river. They were considered a hazard to river traffic and finally removed by the German government in 1976. The "Dwarf's Hole" railroad tunnel under the Erpeler Ley was closed off and used for mushroom cultivation for a number of years and then reserved for seismic studies by Bonn University. In 1992, the twin towers on either side of the Rhine were set aside as monuments. The towers on the Remagen side have been used to create the Remagen Bridge Peace Museum (Friedensmuseum Brücke von Remagen), which features exhibits about the history of the bridge, including wartime photographs and artifacts. Other remnants from the battle survive elsewhere. The M26 Pershing tank preserved at the Wright Museum in Wolfeboro, New Hampshire, is said to be one of the tanks from the 9th Armored Division that took part in the capture of the bridge. The Arado Ar 234B jet bomber currently preserved at the Udvar-Hazy branch of the Smithsonian National Air and Space Museum in Chantilly, Virginia, belonged to III./KG 76 and was quite possibly one of the aircraft that took part in the raids on the bridge.

An aerial view of the Remagen Bridge taken in the late 1940s shows the efforts to remove the last remains of the bridge. The town of Erpel can be seen in the upper left side as well as the Erpeler Ley above the bridge tunnel. (MHI)

A more tranquil view of the Remagen Bridge taken from Erpeler Ley in June 1954. The bridge piers are still evident in the Rhine, but the steel wreckage has long since been removed. (NARA)

The two towers on the Remagen side of the river were declared monuments, and in recent years have been converted into the Remagen Bridge Peace Museum. This photo was taken in April 1954. (NARA)

The capture of the Remagen Bridge returned to popular attention in the United States in 1976 with the release of the film *Bridge at Remagen*. While historical accuracy was sacrificed for Hollywood melodrama, some aspects of the film were well done. Since the Ludendorff Bridge was no longer available, the filmmakers found a bridge in Czechoslovakia remarkably similar in layout and appearance, and the parts of the German flak crews on Erpeler Ley were played by members of the Czechoslovak Army. A number of surplus M24 tanks were shipped to Czechoslovakia for the filming to portray the M26 tanks of the 9th Armored Division. These tanks became one of the more ridiculous excuses for the Soviet invasion of Czechoslovakia in August 1968, with vague mutterings from the Kremlin about NATO presence on Warsaw Pact territory.

FURTHER READING

The capture of the Remagen Bridge is better covered in published accounts from the American perspective than the German perspective. Ken Hechler's account remains the most widely available and was based on many interviews of participants on both sides. MacDonald's account in the US Army Green Book series is an essential reference for the campaign. The Brune and Weiler book, although little known, provides a great deal of detail on the German forces around Remagen. A key set of accounts was written by high-ranking German officers for the US Army Office of Military History as part of the Foreign Military Studies series in the late 1940s, but no compilations of these have yet been printed. This series is available at several archives and I used the set at the US Military History Institute (MHI) at Carlisle Barracks, Pennsylvania. Among the manuscript collections at MHI, the papers of Maj. Ben Cothran, 9th Armored Division, are particularly helpful with details of the bridge's capture. The Roberts autobiography mentioned below includes a chapter on his participation as a young staff officer at Remagen with interesting first-hand detail.

Unpublished studies
Foreign Military Studies (FMS)

Bayerlein, Fritz, *Remagen Bridgehead, LIII Corps*, (A-970)
Bayerlein, Fritz, *LIII Corps (23–29 Mar 45)*, (B-409)
Berg, Kurt von, *Wehrkreis XII*, (B-060)
Bodenstein, Werner, *LIII Corps West of Rhine*, (B-797)
Botsch, Walter, *Bonn Staff-Remagen Bridge*, (B-785)
Burdach, Karl, *The 5th Panzer (15th) Army Artillery*, (B-761)
Hitzfeld, Otto, *The 67th Corps 26 January–21 March 1945*, (B-101)
Kraft, Gunther, *The shooting of my father in consequence of Remagen*, (B-777)
Janowski, Hermann, *Army Group B Engineer Staff*, (B-072)
Janowski, Hermann, *Obstacle Construction East of the Rhine*, (B-105)
Kesselring, Albert, *The Ludendorff Bridge at Remagen*, (A-897)
König, Eugen, *The 272nd Volksgrenadier Division (December 1944–March 1945)*, (B-171)
Loch, Herbert, *High Command Eifel*, (B-065)
Metz, Richard, *The 15th Army Artillery (March–April 1945)*, (B-547)
Puchler, Karl, *The 74th Corps (October 1944–March 1945)*, (B-118)
Reichhelm, Günther, *Army Group B Operations*, (A-925)
Stumpf, Horst, *Panzer Brigade 106*, (B-251)
Wangenheim, Horst von, *The 277th Volksgrenadier Division*, (B-754)
Wagener, Karl, *Army Group B*, (A-695)
Wietersheim, Wend von, *The Battles of the 11th Pz Div. in the Rhineland*, (B-590)
Wirtz, Richard, *Army Group B Engineers and the Remagen Bridgehead*, (B-243)
Zangen, Gustav von, *The 15th Army at the Remagen Bridgehead: 23–28 February* (B-812); *1–9 March* (B-828); *9–12 March 1945* (B-829)
Zangen, Gustav von, *The German 15th Army at the US Breakthrough at the Remagen Bridgehead*, (B-848)

US Army studies

The Remagen Bridgehead 7–17 March 1945, (Research and Evaluation Division, US Armored School)

Col. E. Paul Semmens, *The Hammer of Hell: The Coming of Age of Antiaircraft Artillery in WWII*, (Air Defense Artillery School)

Lt. Col. Robert Osborne et. al., *The 9th Armored Division in the Exploitation of the Remagen Bridgehead*, (US Armored School)

Published accounts

Brune, Lothar, and Weiler, Jakob, *Remagen im März 1945*, (Friedens-Museum: 1994). The most detailed account of German dispositions in and around Remagen at the time of the bridge's capture.

Davison, Glen, et. al., *Spearhead in the West: The 3rd Armored Division*, (Frankfurt: 1945). The classic official history of the division; since reprinted by Battery Press.

Gückelhorn, Wolfgang, *Das Ende am Rhein: Kriegsende zwischen Remagen und Andernach*, (Helios: 2005). A recent German account containing personal accounts of the fighting around Remagen from both sides.

Hechler, Ken, *The Bridge at Remagen*, (Morrow: 1953). The classic account of the bridge's capture; available in many different editions.

Hogan, David, *A Command Post at War: First Army HQ 1943–45*, (GPO: 2000). A very useful command perspective of the First Army actions.

Kurowski, Franz, *Hitler's Last Bastion: The Final Battles for the Reich 1944–45*, (Schiffer: 1998). A short section provides the German perspective on the bridge's capture.

MacDonald, Charles, *The US Army in World War II: The Last Offensive*, (GPO: 1972). The classic official US Army history of the final campaigns in Germany.

Ossad, Steven L., and Marsh, Don, *Major General Maurice Rose*, (Taylor: 2003). A recent biography on the 3rd Armored Division commander with a detailed account of the Paderborn incident where the general was killed.

Pergrin, David, and Hammel, Eric, *First Across the Rhine: The 291st Engineer Combat Battalion*, (Pacifica: 1989). A look at the Remagen fighting from the perspective of the combat engineers responsible for building the tactical bridges.

Rawson, Andrew, *Battleground Europe: Remagen Bridge*, (Leo Cooper: 2004). A recent account of the bridge capture that nicely complements the older Hechler account.

Reichelt, Walter, *Phantom Nine: The 9th Armored (Remagen) Division 1942–45*, (Presidial: 1987). A good divisional history including the bridge capture.

Roberts, Cecil, *A Soldier from Texas*, (Branch-Smith, 1978). A biography of a tank officer from the 9th Armored Division that provides further personal perspectives on the bridge capture.

Tieke, Wilhelm, *SS Panzer Brigade Westfalen*, (Federowicz: 2003). One of the few detailed accounts of the improvised German unit that fought at Paderborn.

INDEX

Figures in **bold** refer to illustrations